# TRUTH

## *IDEAS* IN PROFILE
### SMALL INTRODUCTIONS TO BIG TOPICS

# TRUTH

## SIMON BLACKBURN

**P**

**PROFILE BOOKS**

First published in Great Britain in 2017 by
PROFILE BOOKS LTD
3 Holford Yard
Bevin Way
London WC1X 9HD
*www.profilebooks.com*

A CIP catalogue record for this book is available from the British Library.

ISBN 978 1 78125 722 7

eISBN 978 1 78283 292 8

Designed by Jade Design *www.jadedesign.co.uk*

Printed and bound in Italy by L.E.G.O. S.p.A.

The paper this book is printed on is certified by the © 1996 Forest Stewardship Council A.C. (FSC). It is ancient-forest friendly. The printer holds FSC chain of custody SGS-COC-2061

# CONTENTS

# PREFACE

This is the third book under my name with the word 'truth' in the title, so perhaps some explanation is in order. The first was a collection of classic philosophical and logical writings that my erstwhile colleague Keith Simmons and I put together in 1999, as a title in the series of Oxford Readings in Philosophy. So, apart from my contribution to our joint introduction, it was by no means an exposition of my own views. The second I billed as a 'Guide for the Perplexed', and it wrestled above all with problems of scepticism and relativism, perhaps more prevalent in the carefree 'postmodern' world at the turn of the millennium than they are at present. It was easier then to think that anything goes, when nothing much in the way of war, religious intolerance and terrorism was going on, than it is now, when they are pervasive features of everyday life. In that book I took to task some philosophers, particularly Richard Rorty and Donald Davidson, who seemed to me to have come too close to a relativistic view of truth. But when fine philosophers go astray, there is usually some truth in the offing, and this book tries to do fuller justice to the pragmatist strain in each of those writers, and to others in the pragmatist tradition.

So the approach of this book is very different. It briefly lays out the classical approaches to understanding the notion of truth, but then devotes the second half of the book to some areas, such as aesthetics, religion, ethics and interpretive disciplines, where truth can seem especially fugitive and endlessly contestable. The aim is to show that a better understanding of all our practices with the notion of truth arises if we take seriously the point of Jeremy Bentham's and C. S. Peirce's remarks (see epigraph on page 4). What this means has to unfold in due course, but when it does we gain not only a new perspective on the old problem of truth, but a new sense of the practices of philosophy itself. The selection of topics is necessarily partial, since philosophers have pursued issues of truth and our attempts to find it in more areas than I have space to talk about. Perceptual judgement, mathematical investigations, scientific truth, truth about possibilities and necessities, give rise to their own huge literatures. But in order to avoid superficial treatments of too many things I have instead tried to follow a particular thread, to see where it takes us in a limited number of especially contentious areas. I hope it will be evident how the thread can be extended further, and it will be an exercise for the reader to think about that. Philosophy, like gardening, needs to be practised to be understood, and although I hope to provide tips, suggestions and examples to follow, the point has to be to initiate a process, not to deliver a finished product. To whet people's appetites, I might say that this is also the moral I am deriving from Bentham and Peirce.

I have been indebted over the years to many colleagues, friends and writings. I would like particularly to mention Edward Craig, Allan Gibbard, Robert Kraut, Huw Price and Michael Williams, who have all influenced the way I think about these things. I owe a great deal to Chris Hookway's and Cheryl Misak's work on the American pragmatist tradition. I owe the stimulus to think about truth in law to Andrew Stumff Morrison, and the fascinating, and to me new, material on Thomas Hobbes to Thomas Holden. I owe thanks to Catherine Clarke for encouragement, and to John Davey for his faith in the project.

Stretching his hand up to reach the stars, too often man forgets the flowers at his feet.

Jeremy Bentham[1]

We must not begin by talking of pure ideas – vagabond thoughts that tramp the public highways without any human habitation – but must begin with men and their conversation.

C. S. Peirce[2]

# PART I
## THE CLASSIC APPROACHES

There is an air of divinity that hangs over the concept of truth. Truth is the goal of enquiry, the aim of experiment, the standard signalling the difference between it being right to believe something, and wrong to do so. We must court it, for in its absence we are bewildered or lost or may even be facing the wrong way, on the wrong track altogether. Deception is an insult to this divinity, as well as an insult to its target. Sometimes, perhaps more often than we think, truth hides itself, and we have to put up with simplifications, models, idealisations, analogies, metaphors and even myths and fictions. These may be useful, but we think of them as only at best paving the way to the altar of truth. Sometimes we have to settle for mere opinion or guesswork, but the god of truth is better served by attendant deities, such as reason, justification and objectivity. Once we have it, truth radiates benefits such as knowledge and, perhaps most notably, success in coping with the world.

It is theology that tries, with doubtful success, to unravel the nature of other deities, but it is philosophy that wrestles with the nature of truth. How does it set about doing so?

# 1

## CORRESPONDENCE

A good map corresponds with the landscape. If, in accordance with the mapping conventions, there is a symbol showing a road at some place, then there is a road there, if it shows a river, then there is a river, and so on. The conventions are not always obvious. We may not even know which bit of land the map is describing (think of pirates' treasure maps), and we may not know the conventions. A short red line does not look much like a road, and a thin blue line not much like a river, and some maps ignore conventions that others use. Famously, the distances shown between stations on the classic London Underground map do not correspond with the actual distances on the ground in a systematic way, whereas on most maps they do. Hence reading a map is a skill that needs teaching. But once the conventions are understood, a good map will correspond with what is found on the ground. A good portrait corresponds with a face even more readily, since a portrait can look significantly like a face – one might even mistake one for the other in a bad light – whereas a map does not generally look like a landscape. Both, of course, can go wrong. Bad maps or portraits do not correspond with their target in the way they should.

What kinds of thing are true? For the purposes of our investigation we shall put aside the sense in which a friend might be true (i.e. loyal) or a ruler might be true (i.e. straight). We are concerned here only with the things that we assert or think. They are standardly conveyed by indicative sentences, which we use to claim that something *is* the case. We could say that it is the beliefs expressed by such sentences that are true, or perhaps the thoughts or assertions or judgements or propositions. Questions are not themselves true or false, although they may be answered truly or falsely. Nor are injunctions or commands, although they may be obeyed or disobeyed. If we think of thoughts as being true or false we should also notice that a thought might be entertained without being asserted. I might wonder whether someone eats meat, and then, discovering that he does, assert the very same thought about which I had been undecided. Unless it is asserted, a thought is not at fault for being false – we can while away time pleasurably enough entertaining thoughts that are not true – but an assertion or belief is supposed to be true, and at fault if it is not. So in what follows I shall talk about beliefs and assertions as the primary candidates for being true or not. A belief is said to be identified by its content, which is roughly the sum total of what makes it true or false.

Beliefs in this sense are public property. I can believe the same thing that you believe, and the possibility of communication depends upon that. Beliefs can also be held in common by people speaking different languages, although there can be difficulties of exact translation. To investigate truth I am going to put aside the question of whether there could be inexpressible beliefs, that is, that have no linguistic vehicle. People are often led to suppose that there are because of the experience of being at a loss for words, of thinking that there is something to be said but not knowing what it is. However, when we are in that frustrating state, we are casting around for something to say, which is just the same as casting around for something to believe. In this state we do not at the same time know what to believe and yet not know what to say. Similarly, we may want to attribute thoughts or beliefs to animals, which have no means of linguistic expression. But when we do so, we ourselves can say what we think they believe: if on the basis of its avoidance behaviour we say that a chicken believes some grain to be poisonous, we have found words to say what we think it believes.

The first natural thing to say about true beliefs is that, like portraits or maps, they too should correspond with something. They should correspond with the facts – the way the world is. The view is standardly fathered onto Aristotle: 'To say of what is that it is, or of what is not that it is not, is true.' True statements tell it like it is; true beliefs get the facts right. The world bears them out.

Philosophers often say odd things, but nobody denies that true beliefs correspond with the facts: it goes without saying, a platitude that nobody doubts. What philosophers do doubt is whether this is a useful thing to say, or is more than a merely nominal or verbal equivalence. Anything deserving the name of a correspondence *theory* of truth must say more. It must add that the notion of corresponding to the facts is the key to understanding truth itself, and many philosophers have indeed doubted that. They fear that 'corresponds with the facts' is just an elaborate synonym for 'true', rather than a useful elucidation of the notion. The question is whether we have a good understanding of facts, as a category, and of correspondence as a relation that a belief or statement can bear to them. And philosophers do find difficulty with each of these.

Actually, this understates it. Many of the most influential philosophers of the last century or so have competed to express enough contempt for the idea that correspondence gives us a real *theory* of truth, or explanation of the notion. 'The idea of correspondence is not so much wrong as empty', said Donald Davidson.[3] 'The intuition that truth is correspondence should be extirpated rather than explicated', said Richard Rorty, echoing Peter Strawson's 'the correspondence theory requires not purification, but elimination.'[4] Other giants such as Nelson Goodman, Willard Van Orman Quine, Hilary Putnam and Jürgen Habermas all said similar things.

In order to appreciate these onslaughts, consider facts first. Many people become a little nervous with some categories of fact. People often wonder whether there are ethical facts (given intractable ethical disagreements) or whether there are aesthetic facts (given stubborn differences of taste and preference). These are areas in which the facts seem at best elusive, and possibly non-existent. By contrast we might think of good, concrete facts as ones that fall under our observation: the fact that there is a computer in front of me as I write, or that I am wearing shoes, for instance. But then there is the fact that there is not a lion in front of me (a negative fact) or the fact that if I attempt to walk in some directions I shall bump into a wall (a conditional or hypothetical fact). Do I come across these facts, in the same way that I come across the computer and the shoes? I am sure of them, there is no doubt about that. But my confidence is not given by what I see so much as what I do not see, or bump into. It is an *interpretation* of my situation. But to interpret a situation is just to have a *belief* about it. Now, however, it seems that to come upon a fact, such as there not being a lion in front of me, is close to the same thing as believing that there is not a lion in front of me. And the fact then loses its status as an independent entity to which the belief must correspond. We can compare the map and the landscape, or the portrait with the sitter: here is the one, and here is the other. But we can't compare the fact and our belief, if to hold there to be a fact that such-and-such is just the same as to believe that such-and-such. 'If we can know fact only through the medium of our own ideas, the original forever eludes us.'[5]

It is as if in our mind the fact coalesces into the belief. It is no accident that facts are identified by the very same indicative sentences as beliefs: this is the logic we have given them. It is not a gift of the world, an independent 'thing' alongside the computer and the shoes that our minds are fortunately able to mirror. It is we who say things, and as we do so we use the same sentences to identify both our beliefs and what we hope to be the facts.

Of course, we can (and must) insist that the fact about the room, that there is no lion in it, is one thing, and the fact about me, that I believe this, is a different thing. They are independent: the room might have been lion-free although I had no opinion about whether it was, and I might unfortunately have believed it to be lion-free when it was not. An investigation of the contents of the room is a different thing from an investigation of the contents of my beliefs about it. But this is just to say that the one judgement, that the room is lion-free, is not the other, the judgement that I, Simon Blackburn, believe it to be so. The judgement about the room is not a judgement about people, and my judgement about the room is not a judgement about myself. Granted, but this does not imply that either type of judgement is essentially relational or comparative, fitting a belief into something of the same shape, as it were.

We can come at the same difficulty in a different way, by means of another example. Nearly everybody knows their mother's name. So fix the belief in your mind that your mother's name is such-and-such. Now go through a process of firstly attending to that belief, and secondly attending to the fact that your mother's name is such-and-such, and thirdly comparing the two. I suspect you will find yourself bewildered. The belief does not present itself to your consciousness as a 'thing' or presence. You believe it, sure enough, but that is not an acquaintance with a mental thing or structure. It's more like a disposition. You are disposed simply to answer the question, what was your mother's name, by giving her name. You can probably do that without thought or doubt: the name simply springs to mind. And the fact that your mother's name is such-and-such does not hover into view either, as a kind of ghostly doppelganger to your belief. So believing something (which is the same as believing it to be true) is not a tripartite process of fixing A in your mind, then B, and then comparing the two to see if they correspond. Yet the idea of correspondence seems to require that this is what it should be.

Another way to become uneasy about facts as a category to which thoughts or beliefs can correspond is to reflect on the difference between facts and objects, or even structures of objects. Wittgenstein asked us to consider the difference between the Eiffel Tower, a large, structured object which reflects light and weighs so many tons, and a fact about it, such as the fact that it is in Paris. He pointed out that while it would be possible to move the Eiffel Tower to Berlin, you cannot move the fact that the Eiffel Tower is in Paris anywhere. Unlike a thing, a fact has no location, and no chance of moving. A fact is not a locatable structure. In a similar vein the German logician Gottlob Frege had said 'that the sun has risen is not an object that emits rays that reach my eyes, it is not a visible thing like the sun itself.'[6]

It might seem to be so because there are certainly processes that we call 'being confronted with the facts'. If I blandly assert that there are no potatoes in the cupboard, my wife can confront me with the fact that there are. The process is one of checking beliefs, enquiring into their truth, and well-directed observation is a royal road to doing that. Similarly, if you find yourself worried that you may have got your mother's name wrong, you could in principle mount an enquiry. You could look at (what you take to be) old letters she signed, or court records, or birth certificates. You may even be able to ask her. Such processes can, and often should, confirm or disconfirm your belief. They might lay your doubts to rest. They will do so, of course, insofar as you take them to be what they seem to be. But that in turn is a matter of having beliefs about them. The piece of paper is useless unless you take it to be one of her letters, and the court record is useless if you suppose it to refer to someone else. The person's avowal of her name is useless if you are unsure whether it is your mother who is speaking, or whether you think she has dementia. Interpretation and belief is always required, even as we check up on what we might take to be a simple matter of fact. What look to be potatoes in the cupboard may be no such thing, just fakes or fools' potatoes (and that too can be checked).

Perhaps the best stab at an uninterpreted confrontation with fact comes if we think of bare experience, or pure sensation. A squeak, a whiff or a glimpse can certainly engender belief: that mice have got into the kitchen, that Rover has been rolling in the mud, or that there are potatoes in the cupboard. The interpretation may be obvious and automatic. But it is still required to get from sensation to belief: to the unadapted mind the squeak or whiff or glimpse would suggest nothing at all. The association between that kind of glimpse and potatoes is all too familiar. But it is still required. Sensations cannot, by themselves, point beyond themselves. William James put the true situation memorably:

> A sensation is rather like a client who has given his case to a lawyer and then has passively to listen in the courtroom to whatever account of his affairs, pleasant or unpleasant, the lawyer finds it most expedient to give.[7]

In the philosophy of mind it is controversial whether there are such things as uninterpreted sensations at all, or whether all sensation carries interpretation with it. In either case, as far as truth goes it is only with the interpretation that we even get a candidate for truth. Otherwise the sensation remains dumb, a passing experience of which we may make nothing. As James elsewhere put it, 'new experiences simply *come* and *are*. Truth is what we say about them.'[8] As an aside, it is one of the many ironies in the history of philosophy that in spite of such dicta James was frequently (and with some justice) accused of supposing that, given that they are subjectively useful, the consolations, yearnings or ecstatic experiences claimed by religious persons were themselves a kind of truth, ignoring the point that it is only interpretations of them in divine terms that could be true or false. But such claims, framed in terms of supernatural agency or expectations for the future, are then themselves subject to public scrutiny and criticism.[9] We shall hear more about James later, discussing pragmatism's theory of truth.

Although I think the strongest objection to the correspondence theory of truth is that it is vacuous or empty, this does not exhaust the arguments that have been raised against it. Some say that far from being empty it is pernicious, insinuating a false picture of the way the mind relates to the world. It sees us, it might be thought, as passive recipients doing no more than mirroring a self-interpreting or ready-made world, rather than responsible, active investigators, authors of our own categories and our own interpretations of things. Some say that it implies a 'metaphysical realism' according to which there is just one true, complete, book of the world, and it is our job to read it. Others say that it makes the world a Kantian 'thing in itself', lying unknowably beyond the categories that our minds shape in order to deal with it, and so opens the door to a complete and unanswerable scepticism. It would be a long business to work out what justice, if any, there is in these complaints. One thing, however is clear enough, which is that a correspondence theory of truth cannot be charged both with being entirely empty and with being horribly misleading. You can mount one charge or the other but not both. If it is vacuous, then it can't be dangerous. Similarly, if it is vacuous it cannot best apply to some kinds of judgement, such as common-sense remarks about the environment, and not to others, such as ethical or aesthetic judgements.

# 2

## COHERENCE

As I've described, these difficulties about what is involved in 'being confronted with the facts' have left many philosophers disenchanted with taking correspondence as a key to understanding truth. Instead they emphasise the work of the mind in actively interpreting any data of the senses in the light of whatever endowment of categories and thoughts have been developed by long processes of experience and learning. If we go back to the subject intent on allaying doubts about their mother's name, we see that the simplest enquiry into the truth of a belief will require other interpretations, other beliefs, until either sooner or later doubt can be laid to rest. The hope is that only one coherent picture emerges, with the discovery of signed letters, court records, testimony, recognition, all coming together to vindicate just one answer. And of course, if we are unlucky this does not happen. The enquiry may fail and doubts persist. But often enough the process works, and only one verdict emerges as justified.

So what else could we be looking for? Truth, we surely agree, is the goal of enquiry. But if enquiry must be content with a terminus in a coherent, interlocking structure, a 'reflective equilibrium' in which all our beliefs about a subject matter fit together – if there are no serious doubts that need laying to rest – then why not say that this is just what truth consists in? Why not settle for coherence, which we can obtain, as opposed to the fantasy of a confrontation between our beliefs, over here, with the facts, over there, which we cannot? This is the suggestion of the 'coherence theory of truth'.

We might worry that equilibrium might be obtained although we are completely off track. We would be tormenting ourselves with a vast scepticism, the kind that Descartes raised and which is therefore known as Cartesian scepticism, a doubt that although everything is hanging together yet we may be on utterly the wrong track, living in a fool's paradise, forever shut off from the real facts, the real truth. This is the possibility dramatised as the idea that 'for all we know' we may be brains in a vat under the control of a mad scientist (a mad scientist with godlike powers, since he or she is so good at deluding us into feeling at home). There are arguments that this is not even a bare remote possibility, but for the moment we can content ourselves with the remark that except perhaps in certain areas, which we shall come to in due course, such sceptical thoughts vanish in the light of day. As we go about our business such doubts have no place. Even if philosophers entertain such bizarre thoughts in the study, they are as quick as anybody else to interpret a scene as one of a bus bearing down on them, and to jump out of the way accordingly. So coherence theorists regard the Cartesian search for infallible foundations, rocks of certainty that resist the most determined scepticism, as wrong-headed. We must start not with unreal, mere paper doubts, but *in medias res* – in the middle of things. When we have a doubt that needs settling and pursue an enquiry to settle it we do not empty our mind of everything we know and start from a pure blank slate of ignorance. We rely on what we do know, make inferences that we normally make, and assess sources of evidence in accordance with our tried and practised procedures. We warp our overall picture of the world as little as possible in order to accommodate the solution to our doubt.

The coherence theory of truth gained a strong following in the nineteenth century, partly due to the influence of Kant and Hegel, and especially in the thought of the British philosophers influenced by them, known as the British Idealists. One of its implications is that beliefs do not belong to whole systems in the way that pebbles lie on a beach, disconnected from each other and independent of their neighbours. Rather, they belong organically to whole systems or theories of the world in the way that a hand belongs to an arm or an arm to a body: the interlocking system has the character of a living body, an organic whole in which each part gains its value precisely by its being a part of the whole. This idea, called the holism of belief systems, diverts attention from the single sentence expressing a single truth, to whole theories or systems of belief. As an illustration, think of learning elementary arithmetic. You do not learn, one at a time, that thirteen is greater than eleven, or that twenty-six is an even number. You learn a whole system and a whole set of interconnected implications and applications, and then, as Wittgenstein put it, 'light dawns gradually over the whole.'

In nineteenth-century hands the coherence theory had a semi-religious flavour: ideal coherence, it was thought, could belong only to the thoughts of an infinite mind, a mind capable of encompassing an infinity of interlocking beliefs, something like God's mind, which the idealists christened the Absolute. Anything like it could arrive only at the endpoint of the progress of the Human Spirit, but like the endpoint of the rainbow that could never be reached by mere mortals.

These thoughts might reintroduce a kind of pessimism or scepticism. Coherence is the best we can achieve, but our coherence might not be that of the gods. Again the idea arises that we might be faltering along on the wrong track, disconnected from the real world. The thought is that however much we may be at home with it, the empirical world of common sense and science is but the appearance of a hidden reality of a different nature. In Kant's jargon the ordinary world of chairs and tables, cars and buses, is 'empirically real' – it is what our senses tell us is real – but 'transcendentally ideal' – the product of the way our minds structure a reality of which we can form no idea, since in forming any such idea we would be back deploying the structuring powers of the mind. This Kantian doctrine gave a satisfactorily pious, religion-friendly tinge to philosophy in the Victorian age ('now we see through a glass darkly …').

There is a standard objection to the coherence theory of truth, canonised as the 'Bishop Stubbs objection' because of an example used by Bertrand Russell in his *Philosophical Essays* of 1910. The Oxford coherence theorist H. H. Joachim had urged that real truth belonged not to individual beliefs but only to the interlocking, godlike 'whole truth' that we shall never obtain. Individual beliefs were only ever partially true, and error consisted in misplaced certainty, when we take what is partially true to be wholly true. Russell urged that if this were so, then 'Bishop Stubbs wore ecclesiastical gaiters,' held with total confidence, would be deemed erroneous, whereas 'Bishop Stubbs died on the gallows,' held as a hypothesis with only modest confidence, might be part of an interlocking coherent story about the man's life, and would therefore count as true. A little history, however, tells us that it is true that the eminent and respectable Bishop of Oxford, William Stubbs, wore ecclesiastical gaiters (they did in his day) and entirely false that he died on the gallows (he died in 1901 at the age of seventy-five, in his bed).

Although Russell's amusing objection may have some force against some of the wilder statements of the coherence theory of truth, it is hard to see it as effective against more cautious ways of framing the view, perhaps most obviously because Russell's thought of Bishop Stubbs dying on the gallows cannot enter into a properly coherent system of *beliefs*. It would be doing so only as the result of fancy. But firstly, although on occasion we may become convinced of things for which there is remarkably little evidence, we do not allow ourselves to believe anything and everything that is the result of fancy. If you tell me you have just dreamed something up, you give me no reason at all to believe it. And secondly, a principle allowing one to believe anything and everything that is just the result of fancy would rapidly lead to hopeless incoherence. One can fancy all kinds of things true: not only that Bishop Stubbs died on the gallows, but also that he died from a surfeit of bananas, drowned at sea, and so on forever. Any of these could equally belong to a coherent fiction, so the coherence theory needs some control, some principle for determining the *right* coherent system.

So a coherence theorist is within his rights to specify a much more demanding nature of coherence. The image to be avoided is that of a belief system 'spinning frictionless in the void', as the philosopher John McDowell put it.[10] This can only be avoided if we can ensure that a properly coherent system of beliefs contains quite serious controls. These will have to be described by 'meta-beliefs' – beliefs about how beliefs deserve to get into the system. And we do have such meta-beliefs. A thought is only a proper candidate for belief if it comes with a pedigree: it should be the result of some processes of enquiry and interpretation that have earned their keep and have general application. Most beliefs get into our own belief systems through perceptual experience (to check if there are potatoes in the cupboard we go and look), or, in the case of historical beliefs, through research into texts and archives. In the case of scientific beliefs there are well-established procedures of experiment and observation.

When these fail we suspend belief, but often enough they do not fail. It is particularly in processes of observation that the world provides the friction and resistance that McDowell wanted. It is when we get nasty surprises that the world bares its teeth, and shows its unmistakable resistance to false expectations. It is here that the idea of brute confrontation with the facts has its home. The idea is that by observation or less direct methods we put ourselves in a state that *causally co-varies* with the truth of what we come to believe. By looking in the cupboard I expose myself to causal influences that will put me in one state if I receive light, smells or tactile sensations from the potatoes, but will put me in a different state if I do not. It is in the light of those perceptual states that I gain a title to authority on whether there are potatoes in the cupboard. It remains true that the confrontation is not entirely brute: my interpretation may be instant and automatic, but it is necessary for all that. Reality makes itself felt all right, but it takes a mind to make judgements about it. It gives, but only to a mind prepared to receive the gift. Such a mind can make something of the friction and resistance provided by things: not only the squeaks, whiffs and glimpses we have already met, but the whole huge mass of everyday, uncontested interpretation that we have developed since childhood.

We might at this point even say that correspondence theorists were at least half right. It may not be theoretically advantageous to say that beliefs correspond with the facts. But it is certainly true, and it would be theoretically catastrophic to forget, that we ourselves *respond* to the facts. This is clear when we think of perceptual beliefs, and processes of enquiry that involve them, including such things as listening to informants, checking in libraries or experimenting in laboratories. The road from perception to interpretation can be short and immediate, or long and winding and fallible, but so long as it is there we have a toehold on the truth.

Coherentists have often faltered when trying to explain the importance of control by observation – what William James called the 'coercions of the world of sense'.

Over-impressed by the omnipresence of interpretation, they have often jumped to the conclusion that 'nothing can count as a reason for holding a belief except another belief.'[11] But that is hopelessly misleading. In the first place, it is not a disembodied belief that is justified. It is people who are justified or not in what they believe: one person may be properly justified in believing something when another, worse placed, is not. And the primary mark of placing yourself properly is to confront the evidence, putting yourself in the way of causal processes so that your state is very apt to vary with the fact to be determined. In this way, apprehending the whiff is an integral part of the justification for believing that Rover has been rolling in the mud. The whiff causes the belief, but unless and until one gets further evidence, it is also an essential part of what justifies it. If the belief just popped into one's head it would lack this justification. So it is not simply my belief that there is a muddy whiff that justifies my belief that Rover has been rolling in the mud. It is the fact that this belief was caused by a reliable process – that is, a process that is reliable in anyone such as myself, who has a sense of smell and who remembers all too well what Rover smells like when he has been rolling in the mud. We might have hoped that Rover would stay clean today, but the whiff provides the friction with the world, just as the bell causes one of Pavlov's dogs to salivate, and means that it is 'justified', in the sense of salivating appropriately, because it has experience associating the bell with forthcoming food. A dog that cannot make the association does worse, and a dog that salivates at random wastes its energies. In the language of the logic of relations, Davidson's mistake is to think that the domain of possible substitutions for X in the relation 'X justifies Y' contains only beliefs. In fact at ground level it contains at least a trio of elements: <causal impacts on person a + experienced interpretation by a + belief of a>. And the range of the relation – the possible substitutions for Y – contains not an abstract proposition or belief but a concrete situation <person a holding belief $p$>.* It is we (or, by extension, other animals such as dogs, in the case of Pavlov's experiment) who are justified, or not, in believing what we do.

Control by experience gives (most) beliefs their appropriate pedigree: experience justifies us in holding them as well as simply causing us to hold them. This confirmation can be very indirect, trickling through complex theory and a web of implications. But at its simplest it just means that the person who has gone and looked or who has listened, and who has a track record of recognising what he is claiming to be the case on the basis of such observation, has an authority that the person who has neither qualification lacks. Of course, none of this ensures that the processes of observation and verification are free from mistake. Even experienced birdwatchers know that it is wise to try to confirm the identification that a brief glimpse suggests, and lawyers have frequent cause to lament the unreliability of eyewitnesses to events. Our default setting may be to accept the testimony of others, but when we suspect that these others may have motives for deceiving us, or are advancing

---

* Put less formally, this just means that Davidson abstracts away from the concrete situations of real people forming beliefs in the light of real pressures of experience, and it is this abstraction that does the damage.

horrible improbabilities, we may be very unwise to do so.

These down-to-earth common-sense thoughts defend a coherence theory against the Bishop Stubbs objection, and they also defend it against the picture of an entirely self-enclosed world of thought, spinning frictionless in the void. The processes by which our beliefs change and are updated typically start with causal impacts from our environment, and when these are surprising they change our mind. If we think it is safe to cross the road, it is the looming truck that forces us to change our mind, and a fortunate adaptation it is that we do so. The words of other people may or may not manage to do the same, and once we guess that someone is advancing a scurrilous story about a good bishop's death just because he finds the idea rather funny, credibility flies out of the window.

What then about the idea that anything less than the whole truth is only partially true? One might have in mind the difficulty of giving the whole story. If we are attempting to describe some complex human affair an incomplete narrative may strike us as slanted or one-sided, and therefore only partially true. We may reasonably worry that we need to hear the other side of the story, and then still other sides without limit. But only some cases, notably those involving such things as distribution of responsibility or blame, are like this. Everyday certainties do not require that we get the whole truth before we get any truth. For example, there are, no doubt, many ways in which my own armoury of beliefs falls short of ideal. I do not know that they all hang together as well as I would like, and there are certainly things I do not know and could learn. We none of us have infinite minds, and neither are we infallible. All the same, my belief that, for instance, my name is Simon is not 'partially true', whatever that might mean (Simone? Salmon?). It is wholly and incontrovertibly true, done and dusted. I know it to be true, and so do many other people. It is ground we can stand on. A professed doubt about it would be unreal, a mere paper doubt.

We can call this kind of controlled coherence, when a belief system together with the principles whereby beliefs have a title to being in the system hang together, rounded or complete coherence, and in spite of Russell it has a lot going for it as a theory of truth. When rounded coherence fails, it leaves the believer no legitimate claim to have got hold of the truth. When a person apparently arbitrarily elects to believe some guru or some text or piece of evidence, and to ignore others, they lose any rounded coherence: this is the problem facing doctrinaire religious fundamentalism. If someone thinks the earth is around six thousand years old, we have to ask why they jettison huge amounts of science, history, and principles of weighing evidence that, inevitably, they normally rely upon, and ignore them in just this context and just this way. We are unlikely to get a satisfactory answer, and insofar as they have to duck and weave to escape outright incoherence and contradiction, their view loses any credibility.

Finally, what about the fear that our rounded, coherent view of the world may be forever cut off from reality, the fear dramatised as the idea that, for all we know, we may be brains in vats? Philosophers have sometimes hoped to prove that there is not even a remote, bare, logical possibility that we are wrong in all the basic tenets of our world view. One simple argument is that we could never verify that this is so, and we should not countenance unverifiable possibilities. That sounds a little swift. A more popular and more devious argument derives from what is needed to understand a world view or 'conceptual scheme' in the first place. Donald Davidson (again) influentially argued that in order to identify what language a group is using we must deploy a 'principle of charity' supposing that by and large they believe what is true and desire what is good for them. Otherwise the process of interpretation could never get started. The argument continues, roughly, that the same principle applies if others are bent on interpreting us: hence no proper process of interpretation could ever describe us as wrong about our world, root and branch. And if no proper process could deliver this result we may assume that such a conclusion – that we have so misunderstood our world – must be false. It is safe to say that no such argument is uncontroversial: the possibility of a wholly Matrix-like existence in a virtual reality has too much imaginative bite to be exorcised so easily.

So in spite of its virtues, there remain lingering doubts as to whether even rounded coherence is enough. We may still be troubled by the possibility of a large, roundly coherent body of belief that is, for all that, a giant fiction, an elaborate fairy story. One way of fending off this threat might be to bring in an aspect of truth that is so far missing: its connection with successful action.

# 3

## PRAGMATISM

When we are out of touch with the way things work we are set to fail in our actions, but when we know our way about we succeed. Success is a mark that we are getting things right; failure denotes that we have not done so. The associations are not perfect: we can understand a mechanism but fail to use it appropriately, for example through carelessness, and, conversely, a false belief can bring about a successful action, for instance by luck. But overall, in countless ways, day in and day out, we can do what we want to do because we are familiar with the way things are. I would not be as good as I am at getting to my office if I was wrong about the layout of Cambridge; I would not succeed in pulling on my trousers if I was wrong about them having two legs.

A coherence theorist need not regard a criterion of success in action as a competitor to his own view. Indeed, he can deny that it really brings in any new element. A rounded coherent system of beliefs will include many beliefs about our own successes – such as my belief that I have for many years got to my office successfully. But it is the success itself that causes my belief that I am successful, and that dissolves any temptation to scepticism. At the end of the twentieth century the intellectual fashion known as postmodernism took an ironical stance towards science, regarding it in an anthropological spirit as simply the ideology of a particular tribe of self-selecting people calling themselves physicists, chemists, engineers or biologists. The standpoint seemed to many to be a sophisticated response to science's claims to authority. It was tough-minded and knowing, and its proponents could flatter themselves as having seen through and exploded spurious claims to authority, as relativists and sceptics typically do. It was all very exciting – until one saw the same sophisticates using iPhones and GPS devices, relying on detergents and paints and aeroplanes, vaccinating their children and doing all the other things that the progress of science has enabled us to do. And then its glamour disappears, and instead it looks more than a little bonkers. You risk a certain amount of ridicule if you hope to undermine science's claims to deliver true, or largely true, theories while at the same time relying happily on so many things designed in the light of those theories. Knowing how things work is surely close to knowing how to use them for our own purposes, and if the sciences deliver this latter, it seems graceless to deny them the former. At the very least abundant success must show that they are on the right track: the proof of the pudding is in the eating. A fully rounded coherence requires a concord between what we believe and how we act. This is what the fanatic in his desert hideout, using a bank account accessed with a mobile phone to plot the overthrow of western civilisation and its entire works, conspicuously lacks.

The connection between true belief and success is further cemented if we indulge in a little evolutionary thinking. Our big brains are notoriously expensive to run, so why has evolution burdened us with them? The natural answer is that they enable us to cope. By thinking, we learn how to overcome obstacles, invent new strategies, make use of new technologies.

Nor is this confined to humans. Throughout nature cognition is at the service of action. Thus, in his observation of honeybees, Karl von Frisch was able to interpret aspects of bees' dances as signals telling of the presence of food, its distance and its direction, by correlating the behaviour with the successes bees have in directing other members of the hive to fly in the right way. If there had been no consequential behaviours, there would have been no interpretation of their movements. We surmise that the bees have the aim of collecting nectar, since this is how they live, and Frisch discovered the communication process enabling them to do so, with features of the signal directing features of their journey to food. The connection between cognition, as awareness of truths, and the role it has in enabling actions that fulfil our desires or needs is summarised in dicta voiced in various ways by various philosophers: reason is the slave of the passions (David Hume) or a belief is a preparation for action (Alexander Bain). We want true beliefs largely because we want to act successfully.

This connection between truth and success in action was the watchword of the 'American pragmatists', a group of philosophers that emerged in the last twenty years or so of the nineteenth century, whose leading members included C. S. Peirce, William James and John Dewey. They do not form an indivisible whole, but the tenor of the approach is unmistakable:

> The true is the opposite of whatever is instable, of whatever is
> practically disappointing, of whatever is useless, of whatever
> is lying and unreliable, of whatever is unverifiable and
> unsupported, of whatever is inconsistent and contradictory,
> of whatever is artificial and eccentric, of whatever is unreal
> in the sense of being of no practical account …What wonder
> that its very name awakens loyal feeling![12]

James's verve as a writer often led him to somewhat scatter-shot formulations, as here, and we shall come upon some of the trouble this caused. C. S. Peirce had offered a more cautious formulation in a famous essay.[13] Peirce was interested in the way in which scientists, although they may begin by holding different theories, or wanting to approach phenomena in different ways, will be led to converge: 'the progress of investigation carries them by a force outside of themselves to one and the same conclusion.' He compared this force to an operation of destiny:

> No modification of the point of view taken, no selection
> of other facts for study, no natural bent of mind even, can
> enable a man to escape the predestinate opinion. This great
> law is embodied in the conception of truth and reality. The
> opinion which is fated to be ultimately agreed to by all who
> investigate, is what we mean by the truth, and the object
> represented in this opinion is the real. (pp. 56–7)

Thought of as a definition of truth, this is subject to damning criticism: there are surely truths that we may be condemned never to discover. The 'long run' of investigation may not be all that long, if catastrophe overtakes the entire scientific community, so there may be nothing that is fated to be ultimately agreed upon. We could slacken the description a little to meet this problem, substituting that a truth is something that *would* be agreed by all who investigate, if they were to do so long enough, but making no claim that anybody will actually be able to do that. Still, even if we did arrive at the end of the long run of investigation, we would not know that we were there. The posit that we are finished would itself be unverifiable. But scholars agree that Peirce was not advancing the final quoted sentence as a definition. He was not interested in the reality of an endpoint. He was interested in the actual processes of scientific enquiry, and the ways in which convergence does take place, so that consensus also emerges and dissent fades into history. In short, he was interested in process rather than product: the actual procedures that winnow out the constraints on what we are to think, and it is when, but only when, those who investigate begin to converge that they can talk of themselves as being on the right track, closing in on the truth. Peirce was not interested in God's truth, truth at an imagined endpoint of enquiry, but in the actual laborious processes through which we are entitled to take ourselves as getting nearer to the truth.

It is, inevitably, not quite as simple as it sounds. Peirce was himself a scientist, largely dealing with sciences of measurement and calculation where it is easy to believe that 'all who investigate' would converge on the same result. But even in scientific contexts there are cases where this is less likely to happen. It is, for instance, a scientific question as to whether people can communicate with each other by extra-sensory perception, or can interfere with the physical properties of things by pure thought alone, or foretell the future. Myself, I think there is a truth about all these cases (people can't do these things) but it is not at all likely that 'all who investigate' will converge on this. Partly this is because some who investigate are motivated to do so in the first place by a love of the wonderful and the abnormal, and they may be very reluctant to have that fascination displaced by having to acknowledge the humdrum reality. And then in historical and political contexts the pressure of experience often has to fight with preconceived ideas and pre-existent needs and desires. I think it is true and almost undeniable that the United Kingdom went to war in Iraq in 2003 as a result of government lies, but I also think that there are investigators who will never accept that. Reality indeed presses us to believe what is true, but sad to say, when we want to believe what is in fact false, we have defences against the pressure. People dislike admitting that they have been taken in.

The physicist Max Planck is credited with saying that 'truth does not triumph. Its opponents just die out.' As a remark about the actual historical process this may well be correct, and Planck himself, embroiled in the then controversial subject of quantum theory, no doubt had reason enough to say it. But Peirce has perhaps the last laugh, since today near enough 'all who investigate' or who are competent to hold an opinion accept quantum theory. It is, after all, certainly the most successful physical theory there has ever been. So perhaps truth does triumph. Even in historical and political contexts the passions that stand in the way of many people accepting what is true may eventually subside. Those who are embattled die out, and truth, we can hope, triumphs. But it is unwise to suppose that there is anything inevitable about the process.

William James muddied the water in a different way, and much to Peirce's disgust. Pragmatism aims to tie the value of truth to its role in generating success in action. James identified this with giving the believer the 'fuller sum of satisfactions'. But this led him into trouble when he considered religious belief. For some people, believing that there is a deity or providence with special powers to judge them sympathetically gives them a 'fuller sum of satisfaction'. But it evidently does so regardless of whether there is such a being. We can draw the parallel with children in emotional trouble who take comfort from an imaginary friend. But James did not regard this as a refutation or even a difficulty: clinging to his equation, he argued that in this situation the belief is, after all, true. One of the passages in which he defends this is worth quoting in full. In it James is repudiating an earlier idea he had, which was that 'God' and 'matter' might be regarded as synonymous terms, so long as no differing future consequences were deducible from the two conceptions. He writes:

> The flaw was evident when, as a case analogous to that of a godless universe, I thought of what I called an 'automatic sweetheart,' meaning a soulless body which should be absolutely indistinguishable from a spiritually animated maiden, laughing, talking, blushing, nursing us, and performing all feminine offices as tactfully and sweetly as if a soul were in her. Would anyone regard her as a full equivalent? Certainly not, and why? Because, framed as we are, our egoism craves above all things inward sympathy and recognition, love and admiration … Pragmatically, then, belief in the automatic sweetheart would not *work*, and in point of fact no one treats it as a serious hypothesis. The

godless universe would be exactly similar. Even if matter could do every outward thing that God does, the idea of it would not work as satisfactorily, because the chief call for a God on modern man's part is for a being who will inwardly recognize them and judge them sympathetically. Matter disappoints this craving of our ego, so God remains for most men the truer hypothesis, and indeed remains so for definite pragmatic reasons.[14]

Even in 1909 James's conception of young women might have provoked a snort, and it seems not to have occurred to him to worry whether his own mind might be but the result of a parallel craving for sympathy and love by needy females. Nor did he reflect on the consolations a man such as himself might derive by thinking that male rivals for young ladies are themselves mindless automata and therefore unable to enjoy any triumphs they engineer. On the other hand, there is something intriguing about comparing belief in other minds with belief in the supernatural, although fortunately the first is hardwired in a way that the second is not. All of us except severe sufferers from autism see others as minded like ourselves in a way in which we do not see the natural environment as minded like ourselves. Personifying nature ('Gaia') is a fringe activity; believing in other people is not.

But it is the whole idea that truth can arise from a need (or what he elsewhere calls a will) to believe that is theoretically so shocking. By including subjective personal satisfaction of the believer as the kind of success that marks a belief as true, James has destroyed the distinction between pleasurable wishful thinking and truth. It is this to which Peirce, rightly, objected. Indeed there are signs that James himself was not entirely comfortable. Why does he talk of the 'truer' hypothesis rather than saying that for 'most men' belief in God would be outright true? And what is he going to make of the little qualification 'for most men', even if his statistics were right? Is belief in God to be true for some, but not for others? Or is his idea of God that of a being whose existence varies according to the bulk of the answers in human questionnaires? That way lie wastelands of subjectivity and relativism, not truth, facts and reality.

James's false step suggests that it is going to be quite difficult to describe a connection between truth and success that enables the latter to give us a good picture of the former. Nor do we have to enter the abstract realms of religious belief, or even just belief in other minds (male or female), to foresee problems. As soon as we enter ordinary worldly issues that are remote enough we find places where wishful thinking and myth are as good as or better than truth. Many Scots are enamoured of their ancient wild, free, glamorous and gorgeous Highland past, blissfully ignoring that the glamour was larded on by Sir Walter Scott in the nineteenth century, and the gorgeous outfits invented at the same time by a couple of Polish tailors posing as old Scottish royalty. Being a matter of brutish and impoverished servitude, the actual past would not serve nearly so well.[15] Friedrich Nietzsche actually thought it puzzling that, in spite of such allurements, we do care about remote and historical truth. It is a kind of self-imposed asceticism, for which it is difficult to provide a Darwinian function.

The pragmatists knew they had to cope with this problem and they have a number of defences. One is to insist that the utility and success of true belief does not lie in private, subjective satisfaction, but in a whole array of capacities that truth gives us. In other passages James himself seems to recognise this, defending with great vehemence the objectivity of the pragmatist's conception of truth:

> Pent in, as the pragmatist more than anyone else sees himself
> to be, between the whole body of funded truths squeezed
> from the past and the coercions of the world of sense
> about him, who so well as he feels the immense pressure
> of objective control under which our minds perform their
> operations?[16]

A false belief stands ready to wreck any number of projects. There is no limit to the ways in which a falsehood, by worming its way in among the holistic system of our beliefs, can bring us into sharp collision with the world. The belief that I am the most popular boy in the class may give me a sense of pleasure, but if I am not, there are many ways in which the truth can come out and disrupt my fantasy. The belief that I am a good rock climber may flatter my vanity, but if I am not it leaves me poised to wreck the expedition, endanger my friends or break my neck. Even the Scotsman's happy pride in his glorious history comes up against the 'coercion of the world of sense' when he finds that he cannot enjoy the frost and rain, leap about the heather or even tolerate the incessant midges in the way he supposes to be his birthright.

A second defence is to insist upon the public and social dimension of belief. It is not *I alone* who act upon a belief, but *we* who do so. Beliefs are to be shared and evaluated publicly, and bitterness and disappointment await the vain and the boastful once it is borne in upon them that their own estimate of themselves is far from being shared. It may be pleasant for me to feel vain about my singing, but much more mortifying to find that nobody else can stand it. So we share evidence, advance considerations, and try to coordinate our views about things. We 'divide the labour' of enquiry, trusting those who do it to give us the real results of their investigations and experiments. We try to come to one mind about things. And then James's enjoyment of his belief in God doesn't help. It doesn't work on me as a reason for believing in God: if anything it puts me on the alert, since the most atrocious falsehoods gain currency when people want to believe them or find it pleasant to do so.

American pragmatism is not a rival to coherentism, but an elaboration of it, adding the dimension of success in action and enquiry. Together they deliver many valuable legacies. There is the stress on the interlocking nature of systems of belief. There is the mistrust of 'foundationalism' or the idea that our body of knowledge is built upon self-evident, undeniable principles and beliefs. Even our most sacred principles of inference, that previous philosophers would have dubbed 'a priori' or beyond revision or falsification by any experience whatsoever, began to be classed as merely central parts of our 'web of belief', less than sacrosanct if the going gets really tough. (This attitude was of course fuelled by such advances as the discovery of non-Euclidean geometry, and the upheaval that both theories of relativity gave to hitherto cherished ideas about the structure of space and time.) And as we have seen, even our most immediate and certain perceptual judgements are not 'given' to an unprepared mind. They are interpretations of the world, not its naked deliverance. So pragmatists and coherentists substitute a fallible and holistic picture, sometimes using the common metaphor of the web of belief: a loose structure that hangs together, but with each part testable and potentially vulnerable to alteration or dismissal in the light of the evolution of the whole system. They emphasise that each element in the web can be revisited and tried and tested in the light of the others. But they also stress the unreality of 'paper' doubts and the foolishness of trying to empty our minds or start anywhere else but 'in medias res', or in other words in the light of what stands firm at the moment. As Peirce put it, 'enquiry is not standing upon the bedrock of fact. It is walking upon a bog, and can only say, this ground seems to hold for the present. Here I will stay until it begins to give way.'[17]

It is time to take stock. The alert reader may already have noticed that truth itself has not featured very prominently in the last two sections. Although we were allegedly talking of 'the coherence theory of truth' and the 'pragmatist theory of truth', the discussion quickly slid towards such things as the nature of enquiry, the control of belief by experience, and the architecture of bodies of belief. The two directions in which we have been led have a pleasing symmetry. Talking of coherence we were concentrating on the *input* side: the evidential basis for judgement, and its connection with experience and verification. Talking of success we were bringing in the *output* side: the consequences of holding a belief, and using it as a 'preparation for action'. We can feel pleased enough with our cognitive abilities when there is a harmony here: when the friction and resistance we meet that causes us to change our minds, issues in actions that work better, in the light of our desires and goals. But none of this has issued in a tight definition of what truth is. Is it possible that we should not really be looking for such a thing?

A radical suggestion along those lines would counsel jettisoning the very notion. 'Truth', it might be suggested, has too many liaisons with the very kinds of philosophy that coherence theories and pragmatism are trying to overthrow. It is supposed to be something divine and authoritative, attainable if at all only at the vanishing endpoint of enquiry. It consorts with absolutes and certainties, not with the polite and modest fallibilism that we have been fondly sketching. Perhaps it is inextricably tied to illusory notions of correspondence, and inadequate, simplistic conceptions of fact. If there is no 'given' independent of our interpretative habits and no a priori telling us with absolute authority how we are to conduct our inferences or make our theories, then where 'on this moonlit and dream-visited planet', as James put it, is truth and its authority to be found? Better then to forget about it altogether, and confine ourselves to operating the procedures and processes of refining and improving belief, however tentative and corrigible those processes may be. Such was the advice of the philosopher Richard Rorty, himself a pragmatist writing around a century after the trio we have mentioned. The message had an ancestry in some of the more flamboyant passages of Nietzsche, and found a ready audience in the climate of postmodern scepticism, which we have already touched upon.

Rorty's is one way to go, and in Part II of this work we describe some areas where something like his scepticism can seem appealing. But his attack on the very idea of truth is unconvincing, and well before he came on the scene truth had been offered a defensive strategy that foils it. This brings us to the fourth view of truth that we shall consider: *deflationism* or minimalism. It suggests that truth is, as it were, too *small* a notion to deserve such scepticism. It has a proper backroom role but it does not denote an enemy worth fighting. It also does not denote anything that it is necessary to define. Rather, we can point to the interesting role it plays in our activities and our thinking.

# 4

## DEFLATIONISM

Deflationism starts with an observation that is again due to Frege. This is that it makes no difference whether we simply assert something or assert it prefacing the assertion with 'it is true that'. Following usual logical practice we shall let the letter '$p$' stand for an arbitrary assertion (or proposition, statement or belief). Then if 'T' stands for 'it is true that', we have it that there is no difference between $p$ and T$p$. Slightly more cautiously we should say that if there is a difference it would be one of emphasis, rather like shouting instead of speaking normally. But the important point is that there is no purely cognitive or rational difference. If you believe $p$ you believe T$p$, if you prove $p$ you prove T$p$, if you wonder whether $p$ you are wondering whether T$p$, and so on across the board. We can christen this the transparency property of truth. The transparency property repeats itself: TT$p$, it is true that it is true that $p$, adds nothing to T$p$, just as that adds nothing to $p$.

This transparency ought to strike us as odd. If introducing a reference to truth is introducing a real new property, like 'it is interesting that' or 'it was said by the government that', you would expect a difference. It is one thing to assert that grass is green, but quite another to assert that it is interesting that grass is green or that the government said that grass is green. And if we lay it down that any proposal about the nature of truth must respect the transparency property, then it is going to be quite hard for theory to rise to the challenge. For example, if Peirce had been incautious enough to present 'fated to be agreed at the endpoint of enquiry' as a proposal about the meaning of truth, it would fall foul of the transparency property. For 'Henry VIII had flat feet' and 'it is fated to be agreed at the endpoint of enquiry that Henry VIII had flat feet' are not at all equivalent. It may be that Henry VIII did have flat feet but that no trace of this fact remains, so that enquiry would forever be silent about whether he did or not. The claim that he did so might be true even if it is forever unverifiable, so that for want of evidence it does not belong to any roundly coherent maximally complete historical narrative.

We also get a new handle on the question of whether 'corresponds with the facts' is a useful, theoretically rich proposal about truth, or a mere long-winded synonym. If 'corresponds with' introduces a relation, and 'the facts' denote a substantial thing or structure or element to be found in the world, then 'grass is green' and 'the thought that grass is green corresponds with the facts' would seem to be different. The second says something about the assertion or thought that grass is green, whereas the first does not. It would be as if the second turns one's glance sideways, at the assertion itself, whereas the first directs your attention only towards the grass and its colour. And if we repeated it, saying that the thought that (the thought that grass is green corresponds with the facts) itself corresponds with the facts, we would be turned aside another time, getting yet further away from the grass and its colour. It looks as if we could only avoid these uncomfortable consequences by shrinking 'corresponds with the facts' down to mere synonymy with 'it is true that'. Then we might restore transparency, but only at the cost of losing any substantial theory about truth.

The philosopher Peter Strawson summed this point up nicely. Suppose I say something, for example that whales descend from cows. And nodding sagely, you say 'that's true.' Strawson pointed out that this is rather like saying 'ditto'. You thereby ally yourself with me, in the sense that now if I am wrong, you are wrong as well. You do not adopt a different, sideways position by making a comment on my assertion, as you might if you said that it was surprising or uncertain. That kind of remark could be false even if what I said was correct (it might not be surprising, or uncertain). But just saying that it is true stands or falls precisely as does the original. It is more like saying 'I'll sign up to that.' Or you could just grunt assent, as we often do.

Deflationism is the view about truth that celebrates its transparency. Its core is the idea that once you understand the transparency property you understand all you need about what truth is. Truth is a kind of dress version of the grunt of assent. There are, however, some bells and whistles to add to this core. If the notion of truth never added anything to what is given by making an assertion, then it would appear to be entirely redundant. Why have the extra words if you can say what you want without them? Indeed, in the early days of deflationist thinking, around 1930 or so, deflationism was known as the redundancy theory of truth. But this proved to be a misnomer, for it is not always so easy to get rid of reference to the notion.

The difficult contexts are those in which we do not have an identified assertion or proposition about which we are talking. We may be referring only indirectly to something: 'John's guesses are always true'; 'What Sam said was true, although people were doubtful.' We may be generalising: 'every proposition is either true or not true'; 'truth is the goal of enquiry'; 'beliefs are supposed to be true'; 'Mary is always right about people.' How are we to understand such remarks as these? They are remarks which describe a class of sayings, wide or narrow, and the distribution of truth within that class. But they do not work by giving you the actual assertions in play, such as what John guessed or Sam said. So you cannot grunt assent to what John guessed or Sam said, because you are not told what that was.

To take the first of these, if we knew the thought or proposition involved in John's guess, we could progress. Suppose John's guess was that Mary is three years older than Jane. We would then be able to say 'John's guess was that Mary is three years older than Jane, and it is true that Mary is three years older than Jane.' Then we could use the transparency property to get 'John's guess was that Mary is three years older than Jane, and Mary is three years older than Jane.' We get down to voicing the proposition ourselves, and there is no residual mention of truth required. But that depends on being able to identify the proposition involved, and we may not be able to do that. However, there is something we can do instead. We can offer a schema or template, knowing that there is some assertion that fills it in: 'John guessed that $p$ and it is true that $p$.' If we could enumerate all the guesses John might have made (say $g_1 \ldots g_n$) we could go one step further: John guessed that $g_1$ and it is true that $g_1$, and ... and John guessed that $g_n$ and it is true that $g_n$. But often we cannot do that because we do not know what John might have guessed. This is where a term like 'is true' comes into its own. We can sum up the indefinite and incomplete list we might start out on, along the lines 'John said that $g_1$ and $g_1$, and John said that $g_2$ and $g_2$ ... and so on,' simply by saying 'John's guesses are always true.' We wrap up the indefinite number of instances to which we might dig down, if we can, with a simple generalisation.

A similar strategy helps the deflationist to defuse the other examples. It helps to have the notation 'not-$p$' to abbreviate the negation of $p$, as in 'it is not the case that dogs quack.' Then we can offer:

> Every proposition is true or not true = there are no cases where neither $p$ nor not-$p$.

The right-hand side of this equation makes no use of the notion of truth, but the claim is that to hold the one side to be true is just the same as to hold the other. Of course, this may still be so if we doubt both sides equally, and doubt would consist in trying to find a plausible case in which you do not want to assert either of these. Borderline cases of vague concepts are potential examples: 'he is neither rich, nor not rich – just nicely comfortable.' It is a controversial matter to come up with the best logic to cope with vagueness.

> Truth is the goal of enquiry = in all cases the goal of enquiry is to certify that $p$ only if $p$.

Notice that this does not say that the goal of enquiry is to certify that $p$ whenever $p$. That would imply that the goal of enquiry is to discover everything that is true, which is presumably not what is meant. What is meant is that your goal as you enquire is not to get the wrong (false) result. For example, and putting brackets in just for the sake of clarity, you investigate whether eating celery causes weight loss with the goal of (certifying that eating celery causes weight loss only if eating celery causes weight loss). Otherwise, you would have got it wrong.

> Beliefs are supposed to be true = in all cases it is right to believe that $p$ only if $p$.

> Mary is always right about people = in all cases if Mary believes about someone that $p$, then $p$.

We have to say 'in all cases' because we cannot enumerate all the things that Mary believes about people. If we could, we would simply write out a list of the things that Mary believes, and add that these are all the cases in question, and we would get the same effect.

There is now an interesting twist to the story. Initially these generalisations and contexts in which we refer indirectly to some proposition or assertion (but cannot identify it as the proposition or assertion that ...) looked to be an obstacle to the deflationary programme. It worked, one might have thought, when we have the simple transparency property, and do not find any difference between asserting that $p$ and asserting that it is true that $p$. But now we can advance the idea that it is these very contexts that stop the idea of truth from being redundant. It is, as it were, just because it visits these places that our grunt of assent needs its full dress. It is precisely because we may believe that what Einstein said was true without being able to identify what he said that we cannot do without the term. Or rather, if we do attempt to do without it we get cumbersome paraphrases. This is summed up in the literature by saying that truth is a 'device for indirect reference' or a 'device for generalisation'. While I hold that 'everything Einstein said was true' I may still not know what to think about space-time. But when I learn that Einstein said that the curvature of space-time was responsible for gravity I must either sign up to the curvature of space-time being responsible for gravity, or backtrack on my alliance with Einstein. Truth may be a device for doing other things as well, but this is perhaps its central function.

We started this part of the book with a hymn of praise to truth. Truth is often said to be a 'normative' notion, meaning one associated with norms or rules, correctness and incorrectness, and this is its title to divinity. Surprisingly, perhaps, it now seems that deflationism can do full justice to this. We put on our most serious face and intone that 'you ought to believe what is true' and what we mean is that across the spectrum it ought to be the case that if you believe that $p$ then $p$. Only thus are you a trustworthy and reliable informant, which is how people ought to be. 'Truth is sacred' means something along the lines that, in general, if you do not have sufficient reason to believe that $p$ then you should not behave as if $p$, for instance by asserting that $p$ or entering undertakings in sublime confidence that $p$. In particular, perhaps, you should neither lie nor even, more stringently, bullshit. To lie is to make assertions in such a way that 'he asserted that $p$, although not-$p$, and he intended to deceive you about that' has examples or instances that are true of you. To bullshit, according to the acclaimed account by Harry Frankfurt, is to make assertions in such a way that 'he said that $p$ although he had no regard for whether $p$ or whether not-$p$' is sometimes true of you.[18] White lies, such as the many compliments made in socially appropriate circumstances ('It's lovely to see you!', 'My, you look younger every day!'), are nearer to bullshit than actual out-and-out lies since there is no realistic intent to deceive. They may be nearer still to jokes, ironic utterances or play-acting, where there is no assertion made but only the appearance of one.

In the next section of the book we look at cases in which deflationism has the power to transform or undermine philosophical debates. However, one example of this is appropriate here, since it highlights an important and natural objection that might be raised. Discussing pragmatism, we talked of the way in which success in action is a good indicator of our being on the right track. If the things we design according to the best scientific theory work, then this suggests that the best scientific theory is either true or approximately true. Many philosophers of science have seized on this, and brandished it as the centrally important argument for 'scientific realism'. The idea is that we couldn't be so successful in, for instance, using what science tells us about electromagnetism to design motors, radios, communications satellites and all the other things that the modern world depends upon, if we had after all got the properties of electromagnetism wrong. If we had got them wrong, or if we were mistaken in supposing that there was such a phenomenon as electromagnetism, or if the whole story was a kind of fiction or merely a metaphor or picture, then it would be a miracle for it to work as well as it does. But we should not be satisfied with regarding it as a miracle. Hence we should be scientific realists. This is the 'no miracles' argument for scientific realism.

The question is whether this casts some doubt on any deflationary theory of truth. The idea is that it does so because in the argument, the truth, or near-truth, of scientific theory is advanced as an explanation of its success. In a nutshell, its truth explains its success. But if this is so, then must not truth be a real, robust and explanatory property? You cannot say that the mice explain the hole in the cheese unless you believe in real live causally efficacious mice, capable of making holes in cheese. You cannot explain the behaviour of a magnet by citing the repulsive power of electromagnetic fields unless you believe in electromagnetic fields and their repulsive power. In other words, if a property or relation enters into explanations then that is a gold-standard sign of its reality, in the eyes of those advancing the explanations. But, the argument continues, the no-miracles demand means that we have to explain scientific success by the truth or near-truth of scientific theories. So 'truth or near-truth' is in good standing as a real, substantive, causally active property of things. But this is just what deflationism denies. It claims, as we saw above, that truth is just a device for certain kinds of abbreviation, not a good, robust, explanatory notion. So it stands refuted.

Fortunately, it is not as easy as that. What is casually called 'the success of science' in this argument is obviously a conglomerate of many different successes with many different explanations. The success of optical theory derives from what that theory claims about light; the success of mining exploration derives from geological theory; the success of electronic engineering derives from what quantum theory tells us, and so on. And when we disaggregate these successes and regard them piecemeal, we find that deflationism not only survives but actually accrues yet further credit.

In effect, we have already had practice in seeing why this is so. What we are faced with, again, are generalisations, and if we dig down to instances of the generalisations we can do without the mention of truth. For instance, consider:

The mining company found the coal because geology gave them the truth.

If this is right there is going to be an instance of geology saying something which was true and which explains why they found the coal. For example, something like: the mining company found the coal because geology said that it would lie above the millstone grit, and that was true.* We already know how to parse this without using the notion of truth: the mining company found the coal because geology said it would lie above the millstone grit, and the coal did lie above the millstone grit. We may not know exactly what geology said, but all that is required is that there is some

---

* In northern coalfields in the UK, the millstone grit is a layer of rock older than the coal-bearing seams.

definite statement like this.

Similarly for all the other examples. The rocket hit the asteroid because science got the forces right. Science will have said something complicated resulting in a magnitude for the forces; which will reduce to saying that the rocket hit the asteroid because science said that F = xyz, and F= xyz. Again, we may not know what the calculation was, but if the explanation is good there is going to be some specification along these lines, which underlies and identifies the particular reason that the rocket hit the asteroid.

So once more there is a cunning twist that turns the objection into a point in favour of deflationism. Science rightly prides itself on providing the explanations of why things happen, including why our practices turn out to be successful when we follow its recipes and formulae. But science does not deal with the notion of truth. Physics deals with such things as force, mass, acceleration and charge. Medicine deals with drugs and their effects, or such things as surgical interventions and their effects. Geology deals with rocks and their distribution. And the stripped-down explanations stick with the same things and properties that the sciences deal with. In other words, just by being stripped down, they are giving science's own explanations of the success of particular recipes and directions for doing what we want to do. It is good to look through the presence of truth in the explanations. Truth is only present as deflationists say – as a device for pointing in the general direction in which the real explanation is going to be found.

It is rather like hearing someone refer to something, although you do not know what it is. Suppose that, yourself unable to see a tennis match, you hear a nearby spectator say 'I like the way Federer does that.' Frustratingly, you do not know what particular action of Federer's the spectator admired. But you know that there was one. So it is as if you are put in a waiting state or an incomplete state of information. It would only be completed if you learn what it was that Federer did. And similarly 'the rocket hit the asteroid because the physicists got the forces right' puts you into a state of suspension. You do not know what the physicists said and did but you know that there is something, and because of it the rocket hit the asteroid.

We are told that when Jesus said that He testified to the truth, Pontius Pilate answered 'What is truth?'* The deflationist answer to Pilate's question could be put rather pithily as 'You tell me.' Not, of course, you tell me what truth is, but rather you tell me which alleged truth – that is, which belief, assertion or judgement – you are interested in. And then we can tell you what you need to know. For example, if the question is whether the man in front of him pretends to be a king, then that answer would be that this is true if, and only if, the man in front of him pretends to be a king. And it was Pilate's job to judge that, not to start beating around in distant philosophical thickets. To be fair, however, the context may be that Jesus was propounding theological statements, and since it can be hard to see what those are

---

* Often elaborated to ' "What is truth?" asked jesting Pilate, and would not stay for an answer.' The quotation is apparently due to Francis Bacon. However, in John 18:38, which is the original source, there is no indication that Pilate was jesting, and if he did not stay for an answer this was only because he was already himself convinced of Jesus's innocence, and went out to communicate that verdict.

about, or what would confirm or disconfirm them, Pilate's question may have had an exasperated edge, akin to 'who can possibly know what this man is trying to say?' And if you do not know what belief or judgement someone is making, then indeed you cannot know what its truth might consist in either.

The reader may detect that I have considerable sympathies with deflationism. Yet many philosophers have supposed that there is something lacking in it. The fare it offers is too thin to be fully satisfying. The standard complaint is that truth may be transparent in the way that Frege and Wittgenstein thought, but perhaps this is only because it has already been smuggled into the very notion of a statement, belief or assertion. So instead of the equivalence between $Tp$ and $p$ implying that there is nothing much more to say about truth, perhaps it implies that there is a whole lot more to say to unravel the nature of assertion or belief itself. To make an assertion is to undertake a commitment, or perhaps a number of commitments. It will imply a vulnerability: having asserted that $p$, a person may be shown to be wrong, to have erred, if evidence against $p$ mounts and $p$ is falsified. Having asserted that $p$, a person can be held to the implications that follow from $p$, so the vulnerability does not end with $p$. For example, if I claim that someone has a daughter, I am not only caught out if she has no daughter, but also if she has no children at all. The content of the assertion determines the range of commitments with which one is saddled.

These commitments are integral to the nature of assertion: it would not be assertion if the commitments are absent, but could, for instance, be joking. The reason that we find ourselves vulnerable to criticism is of course clear from the pragmatists' connection between truth and success in action. Someone who informs people of what is in fact false not only does an injury to their cognitive awareness of the world, but exposes them to an increased risk of behaving inappropriately, failing in their projects, committing injustice, or damaging themselves. There is no limit to the size of catastrophe that acting on a false belief can bring about.

There are other norms or conventions governing assertion. A person may present what is in fact a guess or a hunch or stab in the dark as if it is something she knows to be true, thereby misleading an audience as to her authority to pronounce on the matter. Some philosophers have indeed suggested that it is wrong to assert anything unless you actually know it to be true. That may be an ideal of a kind, and it is usually appropriate to signal when one's evidence is not sufficient to warrant a claim to know what one is saying. But it imposes an unreasonably high standard of purity: there are contexts in which we assert things when it is pretty obvious that we do not know them to be true. Before the game the fan asserts that his team will win, and although the judicious audience will maintain reservations, they will not criticise the fan for saying it. In religious contexts it may be meritorious to assert as articles of faith things about which nobody knows the truth.

Perhaps less commonly, and usually less reprehensibly, someone might present only tentatively something of which she is justifiably certain. This may be because of a forgivable modesty, and in any event it is usually less harmful to impart unwarranted doubt than to impart unwarranted certainty.

Other social criticisms may come into view neither through what is said, nor the confidence with which it is said, but through other, indirect routes, such as the implications of having said it, or having said it and said nothing else. These were first explored by the philosopher H. P. Grice, who called these indirect implications 'implicatures'. For example, if I am asked about an academic colleague's merits and reply that people tell me he loves his dogs, what I say does not itself imply either that he is good or bad at his academic work. But the fact that I replied this way, and did not go on to add favourable comment of a more relevant kind, certainly implies that I don't think very much of his academic merits. We can convey attitudes, and thereby undertake commitments, by silence, by choice of words, and by selection from what might have been said but was not. That is, I would be vulnerable to criticism, and in that sense deemed to have been committed to something false or at least inappropriate, if as well as being said to love his dogs my colleague was a Nobel prizewinner, and hence unmistakably at the top of the academic tree.

Implicatures may, however, be more deniable than outright falsehoods: it is often supposed to be less reprehensible to mislead by insinuating what is false, than it is to lie outright. It is not all that clear why this is so, but perhaps it reflects the idea that if one misleads someone, that person bears some responsibility for coming to believe what is false, whereas if one gives the lie directly, that is entirely where the responsibility resides. The trusting audience is then a victim, not responsible for their own deception.

The other aspect of assertion that bears on deflationism is that of how we get to understand what people do as the making of assertion in the first place. It is one thing to make noises or to scratch inscriptions, but another thing for those noises or inscriptions to be rightly interpretable as vehicles of thought or belief. There need to be practices of interpretation that are familiar to the agent and the audience, or conventions to which they are parties. Just as a piece of paper must be embedded in an established social practice in order to count as a banknote, so an inscription or noise must be similarly entrenched to be a vehicle of thought and belief. And just as the value of a note may change as the economy shifts, so the meaning to be attached to a noise or an inscription can change as social practice changes. This is not the place to explore the whole subject of linguistics, but it is important to bear in mind that the amazing complexities of thought and belief that language enables do not come from nowhere. The interpretation of any language is a skill that needed to be learned, in one's early years if it is the mother tongue, or with more pain and effort if it is not.

# 5

## TARSKI AND THE SEMANTIC THEORY OF TRUTH

This brings us to a philosophical and logical project that ought to be touched upon before we leave this part of the book. Perhaps the most famous name among theorists who have studied truth is that of the logician Alfred Tarski, whose work issued in what was called a 'semantic theory of truth' in 1933. Tarski's aim was to provide a theory that would give a 'formally correct definition' of the true sentences of a language, L, that is under logical investigation (the object language). This list would be given in another language (the metalanguage) since problems arise if one language tries to provide the definition for itself.* If L is a simple enough language, and only capable of forming a finite number of sentences, the definition could be provided by a list of so-called T-sentences for each sentence of the object language. A T-sentence would have the form of naming or describing a particular sentence of L, and then saying, in the metalanguage, under what circumstances that sentence is true. For instance if L was German, and the metalanguage English, an example of a T-sentence would be: ' "Schnee ist weiss" is

---

* The kind of problem is illustrated by the Liar Paradox, in which a sentence appears to say of itself that it is false, in which case if it is true it is false, and if it is false it is true. There are many versions of the paradox that resist simple diagnosis and solution.

true in German if and only if snow is white.' If German were simple enough to be capable of forming only half a dozen sentences, then half a dozen such T-sentences, one for each German sentence, would provide a formally correct definition of truth in German.

Of course, even in the quite restricted formal languages that interested logicians at the time, things are not so simple. Languages have a 'recursive' syntax, meaning that operations can be applied to simple sentences to produce more complex sentences, and then repeated indefinitely to give yet more complex sentences. So the theory Tarski wants cannot be given by a simple list, and it was no trivial task to find such a theory even for the simplified forms of language that logicians were happiest about.

These difficulties, and the machinery necessary to overcoming them, can be found in many logic texts. From our point of view, however, the question is how to relate what Tarski was doing to the philosophical enquiries into truth that we have been describing. One suggestion, that Tarski himself flirted with, was that he was providing a scientific and mathematically up-to-date formulation of a correspondence theory of truth. But that is not right at all. A T-sentence says, in one language, under what conditions a sentence in another language is true. But identifying this condition is not at all the same thing as relating the original sentence to something worldly, like a structure or state of affairs or a fact, as a correspondence theory would have it. According to our specimen T-sentence, we learn that to judge that 'Schnee ist weiss' is true in German we must judge that snow is white. But it does not tell us anything about what it is to judge this, and what if anything it has to do with any of correspondence, coherence or success in action.

This is not at all to criticise what Tarski was doing, and his work has extended to embrace and enrich many formal studies. He was right that insofar as we cannot provide a T-sentence for each sentence of an object language we do not understand the language, and if we cannot provide a description of the way the sentence is built up then we do not understand the structure of the language either. But he was silent about the basis of cognition in experience and in causal correlations with things, and he was silent about the conventions, rules and complex behaviour that identify a group as speaking a language in the first place. Perhaps the most telling difference is that a philosophical view of truth aspires to say something that applies to any number of languages: that human beings all make assertions, all have concepts grounded in experience, all do better by knowing the truth than by ignoring it, and so on. Yet a Tarskian definition of truth in German would be very different from one for truth in French because the words, the structures, and the resulting sentences are all different.

In short, it is much less misleading to say that Tarski was interested in a formal account of what is needed to define a language, rather than what is needed to define truth.* The account is one that enables an interpreter to say, in her own familiar language – the metalanguage she uses – under what conditions any sentence the object language is capable of forming is true. But it is no more than that. It does not, by

* This is in effect the use Donald Davidson made of Tarski's work.

itself, give any insight into the skills or conventions, the experience or the cognitive structures, that the interpreter herself must possess. She must have such skills adequate to the task, so the resources of the object language cannot outrun the resources of her own language; if they did, she would be unable to say what they mean.

We can see how this induces a certain pessimism about the prospects for a real theory of semantics, or the ways in which words relate to the world. Rather than showing this, Tarskian T-sentences show us how words in some languages relate to things we say in our own language. That 'Schnee ist weiss' in German is true if and only if snow is white tells me what I have to judge in order to determine that the German sentence is true. But it is silent about whatever relations I must bear to the world in order to judge it. That is left as business for another day. Fortunately, it is business we have been pursuing throughout this part of the book, in our wrestlings with correspondence, coherence, pragmatism and deflationism. It is now time to sum up where we have arrived.

# 6

## SUMMARY OF PART I

Earlier, we saw how C. S. Peirce was interested in the actual sifting processes whereby enquiry moves us towards settling doubt and fixing belief. William James similarly described himself as following the great physicist James Clerk Maxwell: 'When people put him off with vague verbal accounts of any phenomenon, he would interrupt them impatiently by saying, "Yes: but I want you to tell me the *particular go* of it".' The 'particular go' of truth is found not only in men's conversations, but in their curiosity, their enquiries, their disagreements and doubts, and their ways of settling issues as they arise. It is a question of the processes intended to put doubt to rest, to result in the fixation of belief. These questions may belong to many kinds of subject matter – empirical, theoretical, mathematical, moral, aesthetic, legal, religious – and in each domain there should be procedures for rectifying doubt or ignorance. Asking for the 'particular go' of truth, William James said that 'true ideas are those that we can assimilate, validate, corroborate and verify.'[19] We need to look at these practices, and correlated practices of rejection, criticism and refutation. To revert to Bentham's saying, treating truth in the abstract may be stretching up to reach the stars, but the actual practices of real people are the flowers at our feet.

This introduces a sea change in philosophy, or, since it is not fully appreciated even today, perhaps it is better to say that it *should* introduce a sea change in philosophy. We might suppose that to understand legitimate, or authoritative, enquiry in any area we must first have a good grasp of what counts as fact in that area. Legitimate enquiry would then be certified as whatever method increases the probability that its results accord with the facts. But as we have already seen, facts are tricky customers. Facts are not things that can be pinned down, and in many areas we tend to flounder when we try to imagine them. Do we have a firm grasp of what counts as fact in aesthetics, religion, morals, history, or even in mathematics or science? What James and Peirce are therefore offering is a reversal of this priority. Instead of facts first, with method analysed in terms of its contribution to fact, we look at the methods first, and then describe fact in terms of the ideal endpoint (which we may never reach) of satisfactory applications of method. The question at the forefront of our minds should not be 'what is aesthetic (etc.) fact?', but 'what makes for a good aesthetic (etc.) enquiry?'

The reversal is parallel to one that impresses many philosophers who think about ethics. One way of proceeding, parallel to that of 'facts first', is to sketch a conception of the human good, or *summum bonum*, and then think of personal or social virtue in terms of its contribution to this desirable end. The most familiar version of this is utilitarianism, which uses an aggregate of human happiness to measure the goodness of any state of affairs. A different way, suggested by Aristotle, is 'virtue ethics'. This asks us first to think of the qualities that enable people to live well, and then to think of the human good in terms of lives spent exhibiting those qualities. It is fair to say that opinion is fairly divided between these two priorities, and it may be that although each has its merits we should follow neither of them without qualification. But it is vital that we recognise and come to terms with the Peirce–James alternative. Instead of 'facts first' we may do better if we think of 'enquiry first', with the notion of fact modestly waiting to be invited to the feast afterwards. This is the reversal that guides Part II of this book. In it we take up some of the issues that arise, and some of the gains that can be made, if we follow the advice of James and Peirce, and ask for the 'particular go' of truth-seeking activities in different areas.

# PART II
# VARIETIES OF ENQUIRY

# 7

## TRUTHS OF TASTE; TRUTH IN ART

It may seem strange to start with this domain. Questions of taste are often thought not to admit of truth or falsity at all. People have their own opinions. A salient fact about taste and preferences in matters of taste is that people differ. In this domain, and others we'll come to, there is a variation of subjective responses, and this makes it awkward to defend any idea of the one true taste. Actually, variations of subjective taste and preference would not matter if we could simply see that some tastes are inferior to others, thereby recapturing some sense of authority and truth. But this too may be hard to defend. The old maxim *de gustibus non est disputandum* – tastes are not to be disputed – is practically a cliché. The thought is pretty much cemented into classical economics when people's preferences are simply taken as they are. None are to be discounted, for they are all immune to rational pressure. Some may be strange, but unless they trespass on the rightful space of other people, in which case moral considerations arise, none are better or worse for that. But this is exactly what makes aesthetics an appropriate starting point for applying the discussion we have had so far. If truth can hold its head up in this context, it can surely find a home in others, where it is of more obvious importance to get things right, and to persuade others to do so.

If we follow Peirce's maxim and begin with men and

their conversation we find that things are not quite so straightforward as the old maxim implies. There exist, after all, practices of criticism. There are professional music critics, literary critics, drama critics, wine critics, food critics and so on. People listen to them, and often respect them, even if they sometimes disagree with them. We may be inclined to scoff: perhaps the critics are distributing arbitrary badges of fashion that their audiences are snobbishly anxious to display (this was roughly the view of Jean-Jacques Rousseau). But before we scoff it may pay to look a little closer. Fortunately, critics themselves have provided ample commentary on their own procedures.

Henry James, for instance, a prolific literary critic as well as a novelist, characterised himself not as 'the narrow law-giver or the rigid censor', but as 'the student, the inquirer, the observer, the interpreter, the active, indefatigable commentator, whose constant aim was to arrive at justness of characterization'. To take first the negative claim, James gives a splendid rebuttal of the idea that it is appropriate for critics to 'lay down the law' in one of his early essays, 'Italy Revisited'.[20] He has bought a copy of *Mornings in Florence*, by the fierce and dogmatic Victorian critic John Ruskin, and is eventually moved to hilarity:

> I had really been enjoying the good old city of Florence; but I now learned from Mr. Ruskin that this was a scandalous waste of charity. I should have gone about with an imprecation on my lips, I should have worn a face three yards long ... Nothing in fact is more comical than the familiar asperity of the author's style and the pedagogic fashion in which he pushes and pulls his unhappy pupils about, jerking

their heads toward this, rapping their knuckles for that,
sending them to stand in corners and giving them Scripture
texts to copy.

James and his friend eventually agree that you can read a
hundred pages of 'this sort of thing' without ever dreaming
that Ruskin is talking about art:

> There can be no greater want of tact in dealing with those
> things with which men attempt to ornament life than to be
> perpetually talking about 'error'. A truce to all rigidities is
> the law of the place; the only thing that is absolute there is
> sensible charm. The grim old bearer of the scales excuses
> herself; she feels that this is not her province. Differences here
> are not iniquity and righteousness; they are simply variations
> of temperament and of point of view. We are not under
> theological government.

In contrast, James presents his work as the student, the
interpreter, and the active indefatigable commentator as
being a matter of opening 'the gateway to appreciation and
appreciation is the gateway to enjoyment.' In a similar vein
T. S. Eliot says of the practice of literary criticism:

> Here, one would suppose was a place for quiet co-operative
> labour. The critic, one would suppose, if he is to justify
> his existence, should endeavor to discipline his personal
> prejudices and cranks – tares to which we are all subject –
> and compose his differences with as many of his fellows as
> possible in the common pursuit of true judgement.[21]

Eliot talks unblushingly of true judgement, and James's talk
of the search for a just characterisation of a work helps us
to parse this. James is implying that unjust, hasty or careless

characterisation is a trap to avoid, and in this he is surely right. The practised eye or ear is sensitive to differences and nuances that the novice misses. An increasing acquaintance with any art form enables us to 'place' it in its tradition, appreciate the problems the artist faced and perhaps solved, bring in comparisons and contexts, and in other words think and talk more intelligently about what we read, or look at, or listen to, or even taste. And this in turn increases our enjoyment, as James promises. If at first we hear a string of notes only as noise, afterwards we may hear melody, counterpoint, key shifts and such intangible features as pathos, resignation, hope, excitement or peace.

Good critics are those whom we can trust in the exercise of increasing understanding. To play this role they need a number of qualifications. Obviously they should have experienced the work, for in such matters one thing we cannot do is pass a verdict on something of which we have no experience at all, such as a painting we have never seen, a piece of music we have never heard, or a book we have never read. A critic needs to have been in the right circumstances: not a hot, noisy theatre, not distracted by other concerns, but able to give whatever it is their full attention. They need a delicate taste, refined by practice. They need to have comparisons to hand so that they can know how this work stands among others in the same genre. They need to be free from prejudice, or Eliot's noxious weeds. We would not usually trust a person's verdict on the work of an avowed enemy or, for that matter, a member of their immediate family (if their child was acting in a play their judgement that it was exquisite might not further the aim of shared judgement). At the very least we would need to be reassured that critics have put such things out of their minds, before we let them hold our hands.

In noting these as virtues of the critic we are following in the footsteps of Hume. After expounding some of the deficiencies we commonly labour under as we come to try to appreciate works of art, Hume describes what we need in order to avoid them:

> Under some or other of these imperfections, the generality of men labour; and hence a true judge in the finer arts is observed, even during the most polished ages, to be so rare a character: Strong sense, united to delicate sentiment, improved by practice, perfected by comparison, and cleared of all prejudice, can alone entitle critics to this valuable character; and the joint verdict of such, wherever they are to be found, is the true standard of taste and beauty.

Hume is not over-optimistic about finding such critics. Nor does he think that the 'joint verdict' is always forthcoming. There are differences of taste and sentiment that are blameless on both sides, and that cause a divergence of taste. He gives a charming example:

> A young man, whose passions are warm, will be more sensibly touched with amorous and tender images, than a man more advanced in years, who takes pleasure in wise, philosophical reflections concerning the conduct of life and moderation of the passions. At twenty, *Ovid* may be the favourite author; *Horace* at forty; and perhaps *Tacitus* at fifty. Vainly would we, in such cases, endeavour to enter into the sentiments of others, and divest ourselves of those propensities, which are natural to us. We choose our favourite author as we do our friend, from a conformity of

> humour and disposition. Mirth or passion, sentiment or reflection; whichever of these most predominates in our temper, it gives us a peculiar sympathy with the writer who resembles us. [22]

Nevertheless, we can to some extent put aside our subjective or personal preferences, and take up the enterprise of the 'common pursuit'. William James, we may remember, talked of opinions that *we* can assimilate, validate, corroborate and verify, and this leaves it interestingly open how far the *we* extends. It may not matter to the processes of extracting whatever enjoyments the arts may give us, if the *we* remains relative to place and time. The fact that the 'grim old bearer of the scales', the figure of justice, is not invited means in effect that we do not have to enter into disputes with people who do not belong to the same milieu. We can raise our hats and pass them by politely.

Is this enough to fend off the cynic, sceptic or relativist who insisted that *de gustibus* … there is no real pursuit of true judgement in these areas, and no such thing as just appreciation, but only self-deception, fraud or vanity? We know that the cynic can point to variations of subjectivity and revolutions of taste, and in some areas, such as fashion, revolutions may follow one another so quickly that there seems no prospect of a 'joint verdict' of any two fashionistas from one season to the next (and there are no doubt commercial and perhaps generational reasons for this, given that the young want to differentiate themselves from the preceding cohort). But he can hardly deny that there do exist qualifications, and disqualifications. Having read Tolstoy in English I can say some things about his work, but I cannot comment on the beauty of the original Russian, since I have no acquaintance with the language. Furthermore, we all know of people who have more delicate and practised capacities than ourselves. I heard recently of the death of a chief technician for Steinway, who was able to tell from listening to a few bars not only which famous pianist was playing but also which individual instrument they were using. I would not offer my opinion against his as to the qualities of a piano or a performance. We are often grateful enough to have things we would otherwise have missed pointed out to us. And it increases enjoyment, as Henry James said, to join in the pursuit of a shared judgement, and to find that our own enthusiasms and aversions are shared by others.

Still, the cynic may persist, however enjoyable these activities may be, and however pleasant it is to come to one mind with others on the qualities of a work and the values to attach to them, is there any reason to think that you are getting nearer to some mysterious aesthetic *truth*? Fortunately, our discussion so far gives us a way to deal with this. First of all, deflationism comes to the rescue. I believe that Ludwig van Beethoven is a more imaginative and wider-ranging composer than Leonard Bernstein, good though Bernstein is. So, I believe that it is true that Ludwig van Beethoven is a more imaginative and wider-ranging composer than Leonard Bernstein. If I voice this opinion and you agree, you can signal this using many words – 'I agree,' 'that goes for me too,' 'that's right,' 'sure' – or you can grunt assent, or without extra theoretical strain you can say 'that's true.'

But we can also say more than this. The description we have given of the just critic, the person of some authority, to whom we might be pleased to defer, gives us an idea of what these processes come to. The good critic can lead James's process of assimilation and corroboration, and this is what validation and verification come to, in this area. We assimilate an opinion when we come to share it, we corroborate it when we come across things that bear it out, and we validate and verify an opinion when we find enough about the subject matter to suspect that it is robust enough to withstand any questions we can think of asking. A good symptom of this, of course, is that it stands the test of time. If generations have found much to admire and astonish them in Shakespeare, Beethoven, Titian or Homer, we can suppose that a critic who disagrees is revealing more about himself than about these immortals. In Peirce's terms, their merits are 'fated to be ultimately agreed to by all who investigate' – where investigation includes paying due attention to those of 'strong sense, united to delicate sentiment, improved by practice, perfected by comparison, and cleared of all prejudice'.

This application of our discussions in Part I also enables us to understand better the point of Peirce's advice not to start with vagabond ideas that have no human habitation, but with men and their conversation (equally, we can describe ourselves not as reaching for the stars but as paying attention to the flowers beneath our feet). If we thought of 'aesthetic truth' as some kind of abstraction possibly lying apart from and beyond all human responses, beyond all our satisfactions and enjoyments, a bloodless property distributed who knows how among the things in our universe, then it would be hard to see the point of coming to discriminate between those things that do and do not possess it, and impossible to imagine a method for doing so, given that we can start from nowhere but our own human natures and all the cultural and social contexts that shape them. Scepticism about the notion would be an entirely natural response to this 'realist' or 'rationalist' metaphysic. But instead we have looked at art in terms of our enjoyments and understandings, and in terms especially of the virtues that entitle anyone to enter into an enquiry or to lead one. At no point are we likely to have exhausted such enquiry – we have a modest (and virtuous) feeling that even after we have done our best there may be aspects of things we haven't fully appreciated. There may be more to be said. But if we have been careful and imaginative and profited from the best opinion of others in the common pursuit, we can be reasonably confident that we have done justice to the topic. We can advance our opinions, which also means we can judge them, perhaps provisionally and in cognisance of our own fallibility, as true.

We must remember that a tentative judgement of truth is not the same as a dogmatic assertion of certainty; we can heed Henry James's warning against inviting the grim old bearer of the scales, the figure of justice, into our presence. If we do we can even admit a grain of truth in the saying *de gustibus* … It may be right that in matters of taste dispute is out of place. But this is not because any opinion is as good as any other. It is because it is collaboration and imaginative discrimination that wins the day, not dispute. Rather than argue someone into agreement, we hope to use persuasion, put things in different lights, to remind them of similar things that have delighted them, or to excite their imagination. It is not a matter of syllogisms and proofs, but of leading another to assimilate whatever response we find appropriate, and this will be a process dependent upon patience and concern, like any process of give and take in which education and learning go hand in hand. As James says, we are not under theological government. In aesthetic matters we are not so clearly likely to get our comeuppance if we are careless, or ill educated, or inattentive or naturally insensitive, as we are if we have the corresponding blind spots in empirical matters. Empirical ignorance implies an inability to do many things; aesthetic blindness seems less important. I am careful to say that this seems to be so: a case could be made that blindness to the ugliness of surroundings, the superficiality and sentimentality of popular entertainments, and the tasteless, indecorous or purely witless diversions that bombard us, is as great an obstacle to decent living as ignorance in any other direction. One can become a campaigner. But often aesthetic conversation will seem less urgent than others, and aesthetic truth less compulsory than more mundane truths.

So far in this section we have considered the practices of criticism. What about truth in the practice of art itself? There is a long tradition of supposing that the artist sees things especially truly. With an intensity of discrimination and perhaps feeling he or she perceives something in things that others miss, and, insofar as the art is successful, manages to communicate to others what it is that they have seen. In his book *What is Art?* R. G. Collingwood, the most impressive philosopher of art of the twentieth century, carefully distinguished between practices aimed at a specific, foreseen end, and art proper. The former include entertainment, which aims to arouse particular enjoyable feelings in an audience, such as excitement or amusement, and magic, which aims to express and perhaps exorcise specific feelings, such as terror or impotence in the face of the ills that afflict people. This is craft, not art, and the practitioners are craftsmen who know exactly what they want to achieve and set about achieving it. A different false view thinks of the artist as possessed of particular feelings that he then seeks to arouse in others. The problem with this is that it assimilates art to craft again. There is a specific aim, to arouse an emotion in others, and the art is the means to achieve it. But, according to Collingwood, this is wrong. Rather, the point of the expression must be to make clear to ourselves, as well as potentially to others, exactly what we feel. The expression is addressed primarily to ourselves.[23] This is why we associate art with increase in understanding. I can only understand how I feel if I can express, or recognise an expression, of the feeling. If we listen to a Schubert song, we not only learn what Schubert wanted us to feel about lost love or hope or desolation, but what *can* be felt about it, or what *is to be* felt about it. The expression lifts a weight, an oppression we feel while our feelings remain inchoate or incommunicable.

However, Collingwood did not rest content with describing art in terms of the expression of emotion. There was in addition the imaginative activity that the artist must have brought to the work, and what the spectator or auditor or reader can take out of it is an 'imagined experience of total activity' – a phrase which Collingwood tried hard to explain, with doubtful success.[24] It refers to something like the sense of life opening up or revealing itself to us through great music, art or literature.* The difficulty remains that if we think that some kind of truth is thereby revealed to us, we face the problem that it cannot be specified except by listening, looking, or reading the work itself; art resists encapsulation or paraphrase. Perhaps it is better to admit that rather than revealing ineffable truths to us, works of art, like experiences of the beautiful or the sublime in nature, leave us strangely refreshed. If we are in the right mood, an hour in the National Gallery, or the concert hall, or reading a great novel, leaves us refreshed and invigorated, ready to face the world and its mundane facts with a new spring in our step. This increase in understanding is not further propositional knowledge (that is, knowledge that $p$ for some substitution for $p$) but an increase in know-how. And knowing how to face the world is no mean gift.

---

\* It also refers to the sense of life being degraded or desecrated by sufficiently bad art. In his *Autobiography* Collingwood describes the awful misery that afflicted him when on his daily way to work he had to pass the Albert Memorial in Kensington. 'Verminous' and 'crawling' are just two of the descriptions of it that he offers.

# 8

# TRUTH IN ETHICS

How can we proceed in order to 'assimilate, validate, corroborate and verify' ideas when we ask how to live? The question is a serious one, since while in aesthetics *de gustibus non est disputandum* has some claim upon us, in ethics it has almost none. If I am minded to forbid one thing, permit another and make a third compulsory, and you are minded to permit the first, forbid the second and allow the omission of the third, then we are in dispute; indeed, in the very paradigm of a dispute, since we will find it hard to live together, or tolerate each other's practices and policies. It is often remarked that 'freshman relativists' – those who hold that anything goes, that in this area it is all a matter of opinion, or that you have your views and I have mine, but let's just move on – are as quick as anybody else to get hot, angry and resentful when they are lied to, or cheated, or given what they regard as an unfair grade, or when their pet concerns get challenged. Free speech (or its suppression), the rights of animals (or their lack of them), not to mention the legal status of abortion or the death penalty, see sides lining up very, very quickly. That, of course is part of the problem in coming at any idea of ethical truth or fact, since, as with aesthetics and religion, we again have the diversity of subjectivities, and again may be unsure how to judge one side to be right, or nearer to being right than the other.

If we ignore Peirce's maxim and simply try to think in the abstract about 'moral truth', it is easy to become sceptical about whether there is any such thing. At the beginning of the twentieth century the Cambridge philosopher G. E. Moore published a famous argument that moral truth would have to be different, root and branch, from 'natural' truths, such as truths of psychology, sociology or other empirical and scientifically tractable disciplines. For example, suppose someone presents the doctrine of utilitarianism, that is, that the value of a situation or the outcome of a plan depends entirely on what it does for the general happiness. This may be true. But it cannot be true as a matter of definition, since it is intelligible to doubt whether it is true, wonder whether it is true, or argue that it is not true. (As a matter of fact, people have argued, powerfully enough, that it is not true, citing examples where promoting the general happiness requires sacrificing some person or some subset of people, infringing their rights in what seems like an unjust manner.) Moore argued that since such a doubt is always possible, it followed that the 'moral truth' could not be simply identified with any natural, empirical or scientific truth. The 'open question' showed that even if you settle all the natural facts, there is still something left to settle – whether one or another distribution of them counted as good. He concluded that 'goodness' was a non-natural, distinct, property of things.

Moore's argument has been much discussed, since although it is powerful, its conclusion seems totally unacceptable. Nobody of an empirical or scientific bent wants to countenance spooky non-natural properties, hovering as it were above the natural world and delivering their benefit in unimaginable ways to one thing or another. How could we know about them? And why would we want to do so? We have enough on our plate coping with the given world of pleasures and pains, happiness, misery, hopelessness and joy. If other moral properties such as 'being good' or 'being a duty' lie outside the causal order of things, how could we possibly have evolved to track them successfully? Evolution favours animals that are successful in leaving descendants, which requires skills in coping with such things as food supplies, predators or signs of potential mates. But there is no story about how success in tracking Moore's non-natural properties would help in the least. And if there is no reason for us to have evolved into skilled detectors of non-natural properties, there is no reason to suppose that any opinions we form about what possesses them and what does not are reliable. Scepticism seems the only possible upshot. For all we know it might be that arranging the biggest three boulders on Ben Nevis into a straight line is the most valuable human activity, that you trespass on people's right by being honest with them, and that misery and hopelessness are the best things to wish for.

Some writers, 'error theorists', take this to show that moral discussion is chasing a will-o'-the-wisp. There is no truth in this area, and if we say, for instance, that stamping on babies for fun is wrong, it is a mistake to suppose that what we say is true. Others, 'fictionalists', suppose that at best it is a useful fiction to say that this is true, although in reality it is not. Either way it is not strictly true that it is wrong to stamp on babies for fun. A bizarre denial, and one it might be best not to express to their mothers.

However, all this pessimism and nihilism is the consequence of thinking about moral truth in the abstract – taking it as one of Peirce's 'vagabond thoughts that tramp the public highways without any human habitation'. If instead we 'begin with men and their conversation', or look at the flowers under our feet rather than reaching for the stars in the sky, things are much brighter. This alternative has its origins in Aristotle, who saw that ethics is nothing else than the business of enabling humans to flourish. And we know quite a lot about what counts as flourishing, and what counts as failing to flourish. Aristotle said good things about this, pinpointing virtuous activity in a life rich enough for such things as civic activity and friendship (although, sad to say, he also had the rather peculiar view that 'reasoning' was the final good of human beings, and eventually concluded that the best life would be one of pure contemplation). Other writers have had a more realistic take on the issue. You do not have to be a monk or a sage to flourish.

In the modern world, the eighteenth century saw the first extended attempts to found an idea of truth in moral philosophy on a science of human nature. The creed of these philosophers of the Enlightenment was that if we properly understand who we are, and our place in the natural order, a theoretically satisfying and edifying understanding of morality will follow on. The giants in this enterprise were David Hume, Adam Smith and Immanuel Kant, although many other admirable figures surrounded them.* Smith forms an interesting bridge between Hume, with whom I shall start, and Kant, who follows later.

In Hume's exploration, our capacity for moral thought has five underpinnings:

(1) Like other animals we have a natural endowment of desires and aversions, according to whether things have a positive or negative effect on our own well-being. These fuel our capacity for looking after our own needs, if necessary by foresight and prudence.

(2) We have a limited or minimal degree of sympathy with others and benevolence towards them, but a much greater concern for our own family and friends.

(3) However, we also have a further capacity to take up a 'common point of view', so, for instance, we can abstract from our own involvement in a state of affairs, or our own involvement with a character, and disinterestedly contemplate the ways in which different people tend to behave. This enables us to take up attitudes to people in history, where our own interests are absent, or even in fiction, when the characteristics of people are presented, even if no actual persons of the kind ever existed. We saw something akin to this when we considered aesthetic appraisal as the 'common pursuit', an enterprise of deciding what *we* are to think about something.

(4) We then have a propensity to take pleasure in and therefore be pleased by and approve of those qualities

* Including Thomas Hobbes, Shaftesbury, Joseph Butler, Frances Hutcheson and Jean-Jacques Rousseau.

of mind that are useful or agreeable to those who have them and those around them – their kith and kin as it were.*

(5) We can build upon this, by means of our ability to enter into conventions, when coordination with others is essential in order to prosecute our interests.

The first of these almost goes without saying. Some classical moralists, notably the Stoics, sometimes make it seem as though having desires and aversions at all is a regrettable feature of the human condition, and one that we should try as hard as possible to suppress. Later on, Kant would show a degree of sympathy with this harsh view, but although all moralists recognise that there may be some desires that it is best to suppress, neither Hume nor Smith had much sympathy with this Stoic ambition in general. Even the term 'self-control' is absent from the genial Hume's lexicon, although he was well aware that it is often difficult to defer an immediate gratification for the sake of some long-term or distant goal.

The second element introduces our nature as social animals. We are able to 'mirror' the minds of others, or enter imaginatively into their feelings. When we do so we may find we can sympathise with them, both in the sense of understanding how they feel and, when appropriate, feeling sorrow or concern, mirth or joy, as they do. The third of these elements, the arrival of the 'common point of view', separates simple likes, dislikes and preferences from the

* In using this phrase Hume is echoing the Roman poet Horace, who argued that poetry is to be *dulce et utile*, i.e. pleasant and useful.

more reflective and disinterested states of mind that under-
lie public approval and disapproval:

> When a man denominates another his *enemy*, his *rival*,
> his *antagonist*, his *adversary*, he is understood to speak the
> language of self-love, and to express sentiments, peculiar
> to himself, and arising from his particular circumstances
> and situation. But when he bestows on any man the epithets
> of *vicious* or *odious* or *depraved*, he then speaks another
> language, and expresses sentiments, in which, he expects, all
> his audience are to concur with him.[25]

The fourth element introduces both Hume's own prime
topics for approval, and his standards for granting that
approval. Hume trawls through the kinds of qualities of
motivation and character that we admire in others. He
makes a reasonably convincing case that it is possible to
identify four topics of love or praise. There are qualities
of mind that are useful to ourselves: we admire someone
for being cautious, or prudent, intelligent, temperate in
her emotions, or herself a good judge of character.* These
are qualities that will enable her to get on well in life. We
also admire, perhaps even more, those social qualities that
render a person useful to others, notably benevolence, generosity, eagerness to be of service. These make a person a
good team player, as it were. Thirdly, there are traits of character that are agreeable to those that have them: a cheer-
ful disposition, an easy-going temper, sufficient balance or
fortitude to take things as they are. And finally there are
traits that are agreeable to those around us: cheerfulness,

---

* Eleanor in Jane Austen's *Sense and Sensibility* is an ideal example of this.

helpfulness, tact, the ability to act with grace and sense. Of course, these categories overlap to a large extent, but in principle they mark different dimensions of excellence. So putting it all together we get that a virtue is a quality of mind that is 'useful or agreeable to ourselves or others'.

The fifth and final element in Hume's picture is in a way the most interesting, and marks not only a major advance on his predecessors, but one of his principal legacies to successors, not only in philosophy but in economics and social sciences. He considers the common situation in which we each want to do something, but can only do it together. So, we need to coordinate. One might think, as philosophers before Hume had done, that what would be needed would be a contract or promise whereby each gives his word that he will play his part. But Hume wants to dig deeper: the power of promises is one of the things he wants to explain. It is part of the problem, not part of the solution. The ingredients he has handed himself so far do not include obligations and rights, and promises are above all instruments for creating obligations and rights.

Instead he begins with habits that involve reciprocity, as in 'I'll scratch your back if you scratch mine.' I will respect the property of others, if they will respect mine. Sensitivity to the difference between those who are cooperative, and those who are not, is found in species other than *Homo sapiens*. A chimpanzee will scratch another's back if the other shows a disposition to reciprocate; less or no such disposition otherwise. So, in a world of limited concern for others we need to expect a reward for putting ourselves out on another's behalf. Expecting the reward provides the motivation. But of course the person first benefited might just walk away, so it is good to have something that cements the reciprocity in place. A solution arises if there is some mechanism whereby the person trusted incurs a significant penalty if he departs from the expected pattern. Giving a promise is a public act that creates such a penalty. Now if the person trusted fails to perform, the person who trusted can expect social sympathy from others, and the person trusted can expect disgrace and penalty. A promise is not a signal of a pre-existent state, but the creation of a new state. And with it comes the notion of a right, invested in the promisee, and an obligation falling on the agent. After we are inducted, as children, into this social process, the institution takes on a life of its own. The mere fact of having made a promise, quite apart from the probability of social penalty, creates a repugnance to breaking it in the well brought-up individual. But it is not only the activities of giving and taking promises that can be understood by the arrival of conventions:

> Thus two men pull the oars of a boat by common convention, for common interest, without any promise or contract: Thus gold and silver are made the measures of exchange; thus speech and words and language are fixed, by human convention and agreement. Whatever is advantageous to two or more persons, if all perform their part; but what loses all advantage, if only one perform, can arise from no other principle. There would otherwise be no motive for any one of them to enter into that scheme of conduct.[26]

Hume's strategy is very much that of the 'evolutionary psychologist'. Starting from a bare sketch of human nature and human circumstances, we are given an understanding of how it is that without any remarkable leaps or remarkable exercises of 'reason', we enter into conventions or institutions that enable social life to flourish. And a key part of the story is that it only takes a basic budget of desires and concerns for conventions of property, promises, law, government, money and language to take root and grow into the most essential supports of our social lives. Hume compares the whole process to the building of an arch or vault, where each stone plays its role provided the others do.

What then of Moore's later 'open question' argument, and the scepticism it brought in its train? Wasn't Moore right that there is always an open question about whether rightness or goodness attaches to any empirically given property, including those that Hume picks out? Well, Moore abstracted from 'men and their conversation' whereas Hume starts with it. There is simply no room, in the Humean vision, for a metaphysically spooky, invisible and intangible property that is mysteriously of great importance to us. There are only the natural properties of things, such as the dispositions of character that make up useful and agreeable lives, and our propensity to admire them, choose them, educate people into them and regret their absence. This is what ethics and morality are about. Of course, Moore was right that any opinion of the value of things can be contested and queried. If someone comes along and says that martial courage is a virtue, for instance, we might well wonder whether it is a quality of character that, taken in human history as a whole, hasn't been a nuisance rather than a benefit, and we can go on to discuss whether in the light of that it should be admired, as it often is.

As with aesthetics, we can discuss what to admire and what to dislike. Ethics is our technique for living, and like any technique it can be practised well or badly. If we admire and dislike the wrong things, we can expect things to go worse than they otherwise might have gone. This is why, as with aesthetics, but with more urgency, we properly treat it as if there is a question of truth to be settled. We do not content ourselves with voicing our reactions ('martial courage – wow!') but are concerned that our reactions get corroborated, validated, agreed and verified in a common pursuit of solutions to the problems of living well. This is why we have the moral and ethical, and aesthetic, language we do, in which verdicts can be discussed and agreed or challenged. There is no problem, in this approach, akin to the problem of scepticism that bedevilled Moore's metaphysics of non-natural properties. There are no non-natural properties. There are only human enterprises of discussing what to like or dislike, encourage or forbid, tolerate or oppose. A 'sceptic' who says that for all we know misery is better than happiness has no voice in any sensible moral conversation. Unless, as seems utterly improbable, he can succeed in putting misery in a more favourable light than happiness, he is not a voice in our common pursuit but a mere nuisance deserving the dismissal he will doubtless receive. Our conversations start with recognisable human beings as their topic: it is we who desire some things and avoid others and who have to solve the problems of living together.

If part of our solution is to agree, for instance, that the convention that gives us the possibility of making promises is a valuable one, then we are in effect agreeing that someone who wittingly and without excuse breaks a promise should forfeit our good opinion. Agreeing to this is, as the deflationary theory of truth insists, the same thing as agreeing that it is true that such a person should forfeit our good opinion – or, to put it in more ordinary language, he did something he ought not to have done. Truths of this kind follow naturally upon the very existence of conventions. Wherever coordination is necessary to our living together, a person who defects from the coordination is a nuisance, and in line for criticism and sometimes penalty. Indeed, we saw above that in Hume it is only with the arrival of conventions that notions like justice, obligation or rights come into view. The landscape before they do is one of desires and needs, pleasures and pains, but not one in which questions of justice or obligation can be raised, any more than questions of credit and debt could be raised in a society without any concept of money, or without a tally of goods and services provided or received. Since injustice only arises when someone defects from an agreement or convention, Hume thinks it is not in play when, for instance, a powerful party (such as European settlers in the eighteenth century) comes across a powerless one (such as indigenous peoples). The former may be under a duty to behave well, out of benevolence and humanity, but there is no convention, or motive to initiate one, and hence no question of justice in the case.

It is here that Adam Smith departed from Hume. Smith thought that anger and resentment were natural reactions to cases of trespass by another. If an agent takes my goods, invades my space, ignores my interests or in any way crosses the boundaries of decent behaviour, then resentment is a natural reaction, and one that a bystander, an 'impartial spectator', can sympathise with, feeling indignation on my behalf. These reactions, of resentment of the injured party and indignation on his behalf by the impartial spectator, are naturally expressed in terms of the agent having behaved unfairly or unjustly. So issues of justice do arise even when there is no antecedent convention to which the parties subscribe. Smith thought that as soon as we have as many as two people, and in a bare social landscape, there are things that would count as trespassing against the proper boundaries of the other. Not only bodily assault and injury, but other ways of showing that, in one's mind, the other person is of no account, cause natural resentment and anger, and any impartial spectator would sympathise with the injured party. By doing so they in effect classify the offender's behaviour as unjust. We lie under a duty to each other from the very beginning, not only after the arrival of the structures under which we live in society.

Smith's rejection of the way in which Hume's conception of justice was wedded to antecedent conventions was taken up and expanded by Kant, who saw respect for each other as a more important foundation stone for morality than the straightforward pursuit of goods and avoidance of evils, or the satisfactions arising from such pursuits. He thought that it was the bare, human capacity for rationality that entitled us to this respect.* Moral philosophers still divide

---

* Thereby leaving himself a problem about animal welfare and animal rights. Many of us will sympathise with Bentham's remark, 'The question is not, can they reason? Nor, can they talk? But, can they suffer?'

on whether Kant managed to make a viable system based on this principle, and if so whether it is an advance on the legacy Hume or Smith left us. We do not have to judge this dispute here. It is enough to remark that there is much to say on each side and that those who do take sides regard themselves as correct and right and their opponents as incorrect or wrong. But we now know to expect that. Each side is advancing something as the proposition to be accepted, that is, as true, and there is nothing spooky in the case, nor anything that should prompt surprise or scepticism. One might wonder, of course, whether the dispute is irresolvable, and one might express that doubt by asking whether there is any truth in the matter. This would be, in effect, wondering whether there is any one opinion that is 'fated to be agreed upon', in Peirce's words. Perhaps there is not, but it would be incautious to announce that at the outset. There is no God's-eye view, or vantage point from which anyone can know in advance the result of the exploration or enquiry.

# 9

# REASON

We should not leave the topic of moral truth without noticing that much of what has been said applies across a wider spectrum. We pay attention not only to the overt actions of ourselves and others, but to the way our minds move. As soon as we have perceptions of the world at all we think about what they imply and what we can infer from them – indeed, a plausible way of distinguishing perceptions from the brute sensations we talked about earlier is that a perception has implications, whereas a sensation just happens. A glimpse or whiff is just something that happens, but when it is interpreted consequences follow, expectations arise, and significances are discerned. And the ways in which people's minds move are as much the subject of criticism and conversation as our other practices.

So what is meant if we say that a person, X, takes something, A, as a reason for some conclusion, B? A first stab would be that when X becomes aware of A it moves him towards a mental state B. Notice that B might be a belief, but it could be something else: a desire, the formation of an intention or plan, an emotional reaction, or an attitude to something or some person. The movement towards B might be checked by something else in X's mind, such as countervailing reasons against B. But X is, as it were, given a shove towards B.

This is a good start, but I think we need more than this. For X may find himself moved towards B but against his will or his better judgement. He wouldn't endorse the movement from A towards B, or try to justify his ending up at B by citing A (he might feel guilty that A moves him towards B, so recognising that it is no reason for B at all). So we can try instead that X takes A to be a reason for B if X does endorse and defend the tendency. He thinks that from the common point of view, a move from A towards B is one to be approved of. He can advocate it in a conversation designed to achieve such a common point of view.

Such endorsements or approvals can come in degrees. At its most lukewarm it might be that X does not actually disapprove of taking a move from awareness of A towards B. Further along he might approve of it, and eventually disapprove of anyone who, aware of A, fails to be moved towards B. He would be holding that the move is compulsory.

The endorsements and approvals in question might be ethical, but they need not be. If someone moves from hearing a politician say something to believing it, one might criticise them as credulous or gullible, and these are criticisms of the way their minds work, but not in a particularly ethical or moral register. It is their intelligence or savoir faire that is at fault, even if their heart is in the right place.

Of course, I have abstracted a little for the sake of simplicity. As holism, which we met earlier, reminds us, any human being becoming aware of something is going to be adding it to an enormous background of things she already believes, knows, desires, intends, and so forth. It may be that a move from A to B is to be approved of against some backgrounds and not others. We may want to say that other things being equal, A is a reason for B, or just that A is sometimes a reason for B, deferring to such variations. But sometimes we think it is compulsory or categorical. It doesn't matter what else you believe if you learn that Y is in China or India, and then that he is not in India; it is right, then, to infer that he is in China. If you believe that there are five girls in the room, and then that there are five boys, it is right to infer that there are ten children. One might say that logic and mathematics codify compulsory inferences. Sometimes we want to wind the clock back, as it were, and use an aversion to B to undo acceptance of A, or of whatever else in our background set of assumptions made the inference a good one. You can be sure that not all these things are true: that Y is in China or India; that Y is not in India; that Y is not in China. But you may not know which belief to give up. So it is better to say that logic and mathematics determine which sets of propositions it is compulsory to avoid. This set would be one of them.

Much of the philosophy of science is concerned not with questions of logical consistency, or with purely mathematical inferences and proofs, but with evaluating interpretations of experiments and observations. It needs to think about such things as our tendencies to generalise, the use of analogies and models, our bias towards simplicity in explanations, and the amount of confidence any one interpretation of things should command. These are essentially evaluative exercises, and can be as open-ended and subject to judgement and preference as comparable discussions in ethics and morality. When we picked up Max Planck's alleged remark, that the opponents of a theory never get convinced, but just die out, we are recognising that some inferential or reasoning tendencies, given what else is in the mix, are incorrigible and ineradicable. How badly we think about those who have those tendencies may vary. When they stand in the way of what we are sure is the truth (or even when they stand in the way of our promotion and fame) we tend not to forgive them.

So we can discuss which movements of the mind are reasonable or unreasonable in much the same way as we discuss which motivations and behaviours are admirable, or compulsory or impermissible. It follows that scepticism about the idea of moral truth should suggest scepticism about assessment of mental tendencies as reasonable or unreasonable. An error theory or fictionalism about whether one thing is ever a reason for another would loom. But that seems utterly intolerable. To say that all movements of the mind, all inferences, all interpretations of things, all tendencies to believe things, are equally good is absurd. If you see an electric plate glowing red hot, it is better to expect it to burn you if you touch it, rather than for it to do anything else, such as shower gold on you or turn into a frog.

Much of our reasoning is automatic and implicit. A perception that there is a chair in front of me leads me to suppose that there is one behind me after I turn round. Isn't it possible that I should have had the perception although the chair was an ephemeral being; a manifestation that itself carried no implications for the moment when I twirl around and bend my knees? Yes, barely possible. But a mind that took that possibility to be wide open, that failed to make the inference, is not one well adapted to life in this wonderfully regular and predictable world in which we live, and in which we have been adapted to live. It would be neither useful nor agreeable to possess such a mind. In fact, taken to the limit it would not be a mind at all but a mere register of sensations of the moment; in Kant's terms, a 'rhapsody of sensation, less even than a dream', or, as William James put it, 'a blooming buzzing confusion'. It is with inference that sensation turns into perception.

When we talk of reason, as when we talk of aesthetics and morality, things become much clearer when we stop dealing with truth in the abstract and look at the 'particular go' of it. We then understand why we want it: it is because we do not want people thinking badly, faltering along foolish paths of inference, and we need to signal what counts as doing so. We remove anything spooky from the area, and we sideline error theories and fictionalism, for both these are reactions to Moore's non-natural distribution of moral properties or moral facts 'out there'. In the case of reasons, they would similarly suppose that there is a non-natural distribution of inferences we ought to hold and things we ought to believe (a distribution that exists somewhere in reality, 'out there'), but despair about our actual contact with them. Whereas if we start where we are and look at our procedures of conversation, agreement and disagreement – and at our actual successes in learning how to live and what to believe – we can achieve modest confidences, although at any time we may encounter problems that stump us. In other words, we locate 'moral truth' or 'rational truth' as the axis around which important discussions and enquiries revolve, hopefully informed by whatever we know and think we know about human beings, their limitations and their possibilities. The enquiry is essentially practical: we can say that its goal is truth, but it can as well be described as knowing when and how to act, whom to admire, how to educate people, what to believe, or, all in all, how to live.

# 10

## RELIGION AND TRUTH

Like aesthetics and ethics, religion is an area whose credentials, if they are presented in terms of truth and fact, seem decidedly doubtful. As with aesthetics, we have, obviously enough, the great diversity of personal responses, as different religions have appealed or continue to appeal to different people in different social and cultural circumstances. They can't all be true. And even under the broad umbrellas of religions such as Christianity or Islam sects proliferate and are all too apt to sow discord and hatred. One man's faith is another man's lunacy, or worse, and peaceful co-existence is a fragile commodity, little more than a short truce in the battles for hearts and minds: battles, unfortunately, in which the adherents of one sect rather too often set about murdering those of another.

One might suppose that this is just an unfortunate side effect, a by-product of our not yet having found the right words or true religion. But it is more than that. The anthropologist Emile Durkheim supposed that the principal function of religious practice was to weld numbers of people into a social whole, a congregation. To this end the arbitrary nature of practices of faith, such as the veneration of some text, or some place or object, is ideally adapted. You gain a separate identity, a tribal badge as it were, by the very arbitrariness. You can't distinguish yourself from your neighbours by saying that we are the people who eat and breathe, but you can by identifying as the people who read just these books or sing just these songs, wear these hats, grow these beards, cut our hair, wear veils, take off our shoes, eat seafood, worship cows, or don't.

One of the nice features of Durkheim's account is that it reconciles the existence of arbitrary systems of faith with the evolutionary pressure to have our systems of confident belief conducive to success in action. If religion is a prime cement of tribal loyalty, then it may well be adaptive for social animals such as ourselves to exempt its doctrines from the critical attention that our reasoning powers order us to bestow on beliefs in other areas. As far as reason is concerned, religion has a get-out-of-jail-free card. It would otherwise be difficult to explain the success of arbitrary practices of belief, up to and including those of the most outlandish cults, in a Darwinian world.

It is vital to the way this mechanism works that it is not recognised as such. To weld people into a social unit or congregation, religions need faith, not an ironic understanding that you would be doing entirely different things if the chips had fallen differently. The mysterious or ineffable nature of religious doctrine is a handmaiden to this faith. It deliberately stupefies the understanding, protecting the tenets of a religion with a shroud or mist that makes processes of rational assessment, weighing of probabilities, or scientific investigation not only ineffective, but blasphemous, even, inadequate to the tremendous weight and gravity of the central mysteries. It is presumptuous and indeed a kind of desecration to suppose that finite creatures can comprehend the infinite.

Perhaps so, but for centuries theologians tried to do better. Until the seventeenth century the most able thinkers in Europe and the Islamic world beat their heads trying to understand God. Concepts such as existence, time, causation, substance, necessity, omnipotence, foreknowledge, infinitude, evil and many others were shaped and deployed and discarded and resurrected in the process. One of the most powerful schools of philosophy in the ancient, classical world had been that of the sceptics, who doubted the power of human reason to fathom issues far removed from simple empirical experience. But their cautions had little influence on theologians, compared with the glittering prize of establishing a true understanding of the cosmos with a definite place for God as well as for ourselves. God was to be the underlying cause of everything, the ground of the being of the universe, the unmoved mover, and the only issue was to settle on his relationship to us.

One of the earliest modern voices to pour cold water on any such ambition was Thomas Hobbes.[27] Hobbes believed that it was natural to people to ask for the cause or ground of the entire cosmos, and to push back along the chain of causes until, out of simple weariness, we can get no further. We then call the stopping point, of which we can have no definite conception, God. Hobbes did not rail against this tendency of the mind, but he insisted that we can go no further:

> He that will attribute to God, nothing but what is warranted by natural reason, must either use such negative attributes, as infinite, eternal, incomprehensible; or superlatives, as most high, most great, and the like; or indefinite, as good, just, holy, creator; and in such sense, as if he meant not to declare

what He is (for that were to circumscribe Him within the limits of our fancy), but how much we admire Him, and how ready we would be to obey Him; which is a sign of humility, and of a will to honour him as much as we can.[28]

Giving ourselves the vague idea of an ultimate ground for the gigantic frame of the physical universe, all we can do is, as it were, feel thankful and grateful, although we have absolutely no idea to what kind of thing or things our thanks and gratitude are directed. Hobbes offers a splendid analogy to describe the befuddlements of those theologians who pretend to offer more:

> But they that venture to reason of his Nature, from these Attributes of Honour, losing their understanding in the very first attempt, fall from one Inconvenience into another, without end, and without number; in the same manner, as when a man ignorant of the Ceremonies of Court, coming into the presence of a greater Person than he is used to speak to, and stumbling at his entrance, to save himself from falling, lets slip his Cloake; to recover his Cloake, lets fall his Hat; and with one disorder after another, discovers his astonishment and rusticity.[29]

It is an inevitable part of the human lot to become thus befuddled at any attempt to comprehend whatever it might be that serves as a cause or ground for the entire cosmos.

Hobbes is usually described as an atheist, or at best an agnostic, but it is not plain that these labels fit. He certainly thought that the sovereign power in a state had the right to command specific religious practices – toleration was a rare commodity in the seventeenth century – and, crucially, he had nothing to say against advancing the right kinds of praise, even if we have no idea what it is that we are praising, except, of course, the vast frame of nature that sustains us. Such praises can sound right to religious ears. They might include saying that God is infinite, great, just, loving, and so on, but we should realise that these are not descriptions of a being, and therefore true or false according to whether they get the being's nature right. According to Hobbes, such praises are:

> oblations rather than propositions, and these names, if we were to apply them to God as we understand them, would be called blasphemies and sins against God's ordinance (which forbids us to take His name in vain) rather than true propositions ... The words under discussion are not the propositions of people philosophizing but the actions of those who pay homage.[30]

In short, theologians might think they are investigating the nature of God (or the afterlife) but all they manage to do is to take up a beatific attitude to the world, and, hopefully, to each other. Such attitudes can have other functions than that of tribal cement, as identified by Durkheim. They can act as consolations, for as the philosopher Roger Scruton has said, the consolation of an imaginary friend is not an imaginary consolation. When life goes badly it can be pleasant to imagine a better world hereafter.

Why was Hobbes so sure that any attempt to circumscribe the nature of whatever it might be that grounds the entire frame of nature must fail? The formula that the finite should not attempt to comprehend the infinite is scarcely convincing by itself (mathematicians manage to say a great deal about infinity). Perhaps the problem comes further into focus if we bring in the next great critic of theological reasoning in the English-speaking tradition, David Hume.

In his great posthumous work, *The Dialogues Concerning Natural Religion*, Hume, surprisingly, has two spokesmen for 'natural religion', which is the attempt to prove the existence of God and describe something of God's nature by means of our ordinary reasoning powers alone. The two spokesmen represent two different directions this enterprise can take. The first, Cleanthes, aims to show the existence of a Divine Architect, a single being modelled upon human nature. This is a being that has plans, designs, intentions and even emotions and preferences. He is, as it were, a human being writ large. The other protagonist, Demea, wants something that exists necessarily, and his proof is to proceed not by seeing the world as analogous to the production of an architect, but by reflecting on an existence that requires nothing by way of support (as human beings most obviously do). The discussion can be summarised by saying that Cleanthes is arguing for the God of Abraham and Isaac, while Demea is arguing for something more abstract, the God of the philosophers. The third character in the *Dialogues*, Philo, representing Hume himself, does little but nudge these two apparent allies towards discovering the size of the gulf that separates them.

Cleanthes's problems are plain enough. Human architects have many properties. They have finite lifespans, and they would not exist but for the previous activity of parents and ancestors. Some are more experienced than others. Some are apprentices, and others are past it, in their dotage. They tend to work together in groups, and they depend upon traditions and long histories of experience. They also make mistakes. Some of their productions are inferior to those of others. They depend upon pre-existent, given materials. Furthermore, if we are acquainted with just one of an architect's productions, all we can infer is that this is an architect who produces things like that. If we have no other examples of an architect's work, or of the work of others with which to compare it, we cannot even pronounce whether it is a good or bad example of its kind. And we certainly can't infer that he or she also makes entirely different kinds of building as well. Above all we cannot infer that they also design the heavens. That would be like taking the multiple imperfections of some ghastly child to be itself a reason for supposing that it has a much nicer brother or sister.

None of these properties is supposed to have an analogy in the Divine Architect. He does not have a lifespan, does not depend upon parents and ancestors, does not make mistakes, does not produce inferior works, does not depend on pre-existent materials, does not serve an apprenticeship, does not enter a dotage, and does not work in a tradition or alongside others. He is to be, as it were, above all that. So it is time for Demea to unroll his less anthropomorphic, more abstract conception of the ground of the cosmos, sometimes called the God of the philosophers. This is to be a 'necessary being', self-sufficient, eternal, beyond assessment, far from capable of being modelled upon the example of human life. Probably Demea's best analogy would be with a number (although philosophers dispute about whether it is right to say that numbers exist). That aside, if we take a number, say the number seven, then it makes no sense to imagine it changing (it is not odd one day and even the next), nor does it depend on anything material, nor does it have a finite lifespan, and it is necessary at least insofar as we can make little or no sense of the idea of it not existing, as if one day we might find that whereas there used to be something between the number six and the number eight, now, alas, it seems to have disappeared. Unfortunately, neither is the number seven responsive to prayer, concerned about humanity, subject to emotions and preferences, a counsellor or a judge, a consolation or a creator.

So now Demea can call Cleanthes names: 'anthropomorphite', making God too like ourselves, just a big daddy in the sky with a whole host of human properties, how inadequate, how blasphemous. And Cleanthes can call Demea names: a God about which nothing can be said, and to whom no prayers can be addressed, how useless, how mystical – and each ends up saying that the other is little better than an outright atheist. But the trouble is that the ordinary religious believer will find that he needs to oscillate between the two conceptions. When he seeks God's help or forgiveness or consolation he sides with Cleanthes; when he reflects on what could possibly be the ground of the existence of the cosmos he must side with Demea. He is in what Hume calls a 'somewhat unaccountable state of mind', having no clear concept in mind, and hence no clear belief or thought to assess as true or false. And, as Hume said in a different context, 'carelessness and inattention will alone afford any remedy.'*

---

* This always reminds me of Alice's remark after hearing the nonsense poem 'Jabberwocky' in Lewis Carroll's *Alice's Adventures in Wonderland*: 'It seems to fill my head with ideas – but I don't quite know what they are.'

It may seem surprising that after all this, Hume, like Hobbes, nevertheless retains a soft spot for the dispositions of the human mind that lead to arguing for an ultimate cause of the cosmos, or a divine architect. There must, we think, be something outside the physical universe that sustains its patterns, a divine maintenance man keeping its laws running, its magnitudes constant, its whole frame capable of supporting order and life. In the final section of the *Dialogues* Hume himself shows sympathy with this tendency of the mind. However, this just means that the sceptic's target shifts. It doesn't matter any more what you say you believe. We are in an area where, as Hobbes said, words function only as 'oblations', prayers or paeans of praise, not as descriptions of aspects of the world. We are not in an area where truth is to be expected. In James's terms, we do not have doctrines that can be assimilated, corroborated, validated or verified. We have something more akin to songs and dances. As usual Hume sums it up admirably:

> In vain would our limited understanding break through those boundaries, which are too narrow for our fond imagination. While we argue from the course of nature, and infer a particular intelligent cause, which first bestowed, and still preserves order in the universe, we embrace a principle, which is both uncertain and useless. It is uncertain; because the subject lies entirely beyond the reach of human experience. It is useless; because our knowledge of this cause being derived entirely from the course of nature, we can never, according to the rules of just reasoning, return back from the cause with any new inference, or making additions to the common and experienced course of nature, establish any new principles of conduct and behaviour.[31]

What does matter is that you should not draw any inferences from whatever you like to say or try to imagine. Indulge supernatural imaginings and practices if you wish – Hobbes thought that a well-ordered state would make it a law that you should do so – but do not think that you can derive any results about what to expect, who to love and hate, what to tolerate or oppose, how to relate to your neighbours, or how to live in general. You have to supply all that for yourself, and whether or not they knew it, this is what the writers of the holy texts – the preachers and priests and imams, and all the upholders of the various moralities that claim religious underpinnings – have always done, sometimes beneficially but often catastrophically.

Might religions, then, be accorded the same generosity that we earlier gave to aesthetics and ethics? There we turned from bothering about the concept of truth in the abstract to describing, and, generally speaking, encouraging, the practices of the enquirer and the critic. Trying to better our practical responses to things is a valuable activity, and recognising that we would do well to look for this betterment is a good exercise of modesty. Could we say similarly that there are religious practices, including those of enquiry and discussion, that can be regarded both as attempts to know how to improve our awarenesses and attitudes towards the universe, and as trying to find religious truth? The exercise could be regarded as close to the practices of art and aesthetics. Just as a musician might be described as trying to find an adequate expression of, say, her response to the arrival of spring, so a religious adept could be described as trying to find an adequate expression of his hope, consolation, gratitude or reconciliation with the universe.

The suggestion is well placed, and there may be religious practices and attitudes to which it is well fitted. A religious attitude to life would be a (good?) version of a well-tuned aesthetic and ethical attitude to life. But whereas it is straightforward to agree to there being know-how in ethics, or grades of experience and expertise in many of the practices associated with taste and art, it is harder to believe that the same is true, or true in the same way, when it comes to a more religious dimension. Beatific joy is one thing, self-lacerating despair another, yet each seems to find an equal place in religious practice. The music of Bach is one thing, and if appreciating it exhausted religious practice all would be well, but the hatreds of sectarians and jihadists are another. Perhaps as the apophatic traditions (that proceed through saying only what God is not) of various religions suggest, a truly religious attitude to the world is best found in silence; but silence is not an expression of any kind of truth, and the effort to articulate any wisdom that silence contains is not apt to deliver anything recognisable as know-how, but more apt to deliver something like Hobbes's befuddlement. Nor is a religion of silence a way to tribal identity, or hope and consolation, nor a provision of moral stiffening, yet all these are things that people look for in their religions. What we find, then, perhaps unsurprisingly, is that any religious practice that seeks a cousinship with ethics and aesthetics, and thereby a title to being its own kind of truth seeking, must eventually stand trial at the bars of ethics and aesthetics. Are the practices it recommends useful and agreeable? Are the attitudes to the world that it enjoins adequate and admirable, in a way similar to those encouraged by great art, literature or music? Is it free from exalting human vanity, or pride, or self-deception, let alone tribalism and sectarianism? If the answer to such questions is positive, then at the very least there is nothing to oppose or complain about. Religious truth could find a berth by sharing a compartment with ethical and aesthetic truth, to which we have been quite hospitable.

But religions are also ways of turning up the volume. A dissenter is not a voice to be accommodated, a fellow enquirer in a serious attempt to allay doubt, with whom we may come to be one-minded about things, but someone to be shunned or extirpated. *Anathema sit:* let it be damned. So looking at the way in which religions implement themselves in the actual world, it would be naïve to be too optimistic.

# 11

## INTERPRETATIONS

The moral of these discussions is basically simple, but I hope sufficiently provocative to be worth emphasising. Peirce, James, Bentham and others constantly remind us of our actual activities, and actual motivations and cares. We only have the language, the resources of thought that we do, because some activities have proved useful or essential. These activities include trying to thrash things out: trying to warp our own heritage of beliefs and dispositions as little as possible in order to accommodate the problems that friction with the world throws up. The language of truth, reason, justification, knowledge, certainty and doubt is our instrument for discussing all this. This language is used in the same way in connection with any subject matter, even, as we have seen, those where truth has proved especially elusive and contested, such as ethics and aesthetics.

This language is also at work in interpretive disciplines, where we try to make sense of a historical period, or a set of texts. An interesting example is that of the common law, which is a structure built on experience and reason. Common law evolves from a succession of adaptations to difficult cases, unforeseen problems, principles, statutes, rules and reasons, all of which are gradually refined by the pressure of experience, and, we hope, better ideas at the expense of worse ones. It is an edifice, a cathedral, especially in lawyers' minds, but growing organically and worthy of the same kind of worship as the divinity of truth itself. Perhaps. Aristotle said that we should live under the rule of law, not the rule of men, and this suggests a kind of structure found nowhere on earth, but somehow casting itself over us from on high. Hobbes, who always had his feet firmly on the ground, mocked this roundly:

> And therefore this is another Errour of Aristotles Politiques, that in a well ordered Common-wealth, not Men should govern, but the Laws. What man, that has his naturall Senses, though he can neither write nor read, does not find himself governed by them he fears, and beleeves can kill or hurt him when he obeyeth not? or that beleeves the Law can hurt him; that is, Words, and Paper, without the Hands, and Swords of men?[32]

In sum, law is the force-backed command of the sovereign.* Of course, we hope that the legislature and the executive show fidelity to as much preceding law as possible, and so require no sudden jumps, retrospective legislation, arbitrary diktats, and so on. When this is so, there is a sense in

---

\* Hobbes's view, echoed by later philosophers of law such as Jeremy Bentham and John Austin, was contested by H. L. A. Hart in his hugely influential book *The Concept of Law*. Hart had two arguments. One was that it may be hard to determine which body is the sovereign, to which the answer is that when that is true it is equally hard to know what is the law – just think of failed states. The other is that some laws enable us to do things, such as making valid wills, rather than commanding us to do things. This is true, but force is close by in the wings, since the validity of a will means that the intended beneficiary becomes the owner of the property in the legacy, which in turn means that any other person taking possession of that property will incur the full force of the law. No adjustment to Hobbes, Bentham or Austin is necessary.

which we have 'the rule of law', and in the absence of this tradition and conservatism (in an unusually good sense of the word) the security that is the very raison d'être of law crumbles. Stability of investment, property and contract, and safety itself, wither and perhaps disappear. Who is going to sow crops if by the summer his property is sequestrated and gone?

It would be nice if we could be sure that later law is better than earlier law, in a rising arc of progress. But the commands of the sovereign bodies, and what the courts manage to make of those commands, emerge from politics and other human motivations: greed and fear, arrogance, lust for wealth, the corruptions of power, and simple fantasies about human nature. Even when tempered by interpretations of the tradition, they may represent a step backwards. So, for instance, the law now gives us a tax code for the United Kingdom that is around 17,000 pages long, and one that has aptly been described as a dog whistle luring the rich into the Elysian fields of tax avoidance. In the United States, the Constitution gives rise to the unedifying spectacle of the greybeards of the Supreme Court wondering what the framers of the Constitution 'would have' intended had they been aware of modern automatic weaponry and crowded urban living conditions. Thus a clause guaranteeing the right of the people to form a militia and bear arms becomes interpreted to mean that almost anybody can own and often carry such weapons in such contexts. It does not yet cover bazookas, grenades or tactical nuclear weapons, although those will no doubt be on the horizon, in spite of the consequence that in recent years more citizens of the USA have been killed by toddlers than by terrorists.*

Sometimes the difficulty of applying rules outside the circumstance for which they were framed are more comical than tragic, as when Gennardy Lupey, a Russian sea captain, pleaded guilty to being drunk in charge of a ship – a bad offence one might think, except that his ship at the time was in dry dock waiting to be broken up, so poor Gennardy had no more reason to stay sober than had he been partying at home.**

Argument about what the law *is* proceeds by citing past practice and interpreting the reasons it has taken the shape that it has. Argument about what the law *should* be is a matter of morals and politics. The two are different, but not entirely dissociated, since our own past laws and conventions will have influenced our sense of propriety and decency, and those in turn shape our verdicts about what ought to be done. But this is no obstacle to recognising the distinction, and recognising that, often enough, there is nothing sacrosanct about where we stand now.

Enquiry in interpretative disciplines such as history or law is apt to be contestable and fallible. The results

---

\* The text of the second amendment reads: 'A well regulated militia being necessary to the security of a free state, the right of the people to keep and bear arms shall not be infringed.' Thanks to relentless commercial pressures and fantastical views of human nature, the initial clause, which clearly introduces the point of the amendment, is now completely ignored.

\*\* The case was reported in the London *Times* on 30 May 2016. Philosophers call the issues surrounding knowing how to extend rules to new cases the 'rule following considerations', which were first highlighted by Wittgenstein.

are typically provisional and open to refinement and improvement or outright rejection. Here truth seems especially fugitive. Nonetheless, it is far from true that anything goes: even when our pictures of how things were are incomplete or partial, they may still be better than others. And even when truth veils herself, falsity can be detected for what it is. In other cases – simple empirical beliefs about the here and now – the cost of getting things wrong looms more immediately, and looms larger. But reasoning works the same way and deserves the same respect whether the question is difficult or easy. And by seeing discussion of reasons as, in effect, versions of the same evaluative exercise that happen whenever those loaded words 'good', 'ought', 'must' and their kin dominate our thoughts, we diminish the gap between exercises of scientific and empirical reason on the one hand, and practical and aesthetic reason on the other. All concern the common pursuit of values and priorities. These values provide us with our stance towards the world, a stance that has us walking upon Peirce's bog rather than upon a bedrock of fact. Here we stand until it gives way.

'I did it my way' boasts the song made popular by Frank Sinatra, plugging into a common fantasy of autonomy and sovereignty. But nobody does it their way, since everybody stands on a huge deposit of history and culture, the work of generations of trial and error and refinement. We all speak a language we did not invent, benefit from conventions we did not design, travel roads we did not level, inhabit buildings we did not make, under the protection of laws we did not frame. It would be as big a delusion to think of oneself as a self-made person in the world of thought and ideas as it is in the world of politics and commerce.

So how can we retain any kind of confidence in those opinions that, for the moment, seem to provide solid footing? The best answer, somewhat brutal, is that we have nowhere else to stand. Imagining that we do would be to go back to the Cartesian quest for a method that requires no standpoint, no landmarks and no luggage, a method that, in all its glory, commands the allegiance of the innocent mind. We do not need, and cannot have, that. We start 'in medias res', where we are, and deal with problems as they arise, deploying a huge inheritance of mental habits, experiences, natural and practised capacities of observation, and inference and reasoning. We deploy our sense of what analogies to trust, what simplifications we can make, what is useful, what solidifies our judgement with those of our fellows whose judgement we respect. Whatever else sceptics and cynics of all stripes may say, we have no alternative. We cannot live without elementary confidences, cemented routes of inferences, preferences, relatively fixed pleasures and desires. These give us the indissoluble rocks around which we have to steer our fragile barks.

And this is what it is to look for truth, to enquire into it, to set doubt to rest, to improve our understandings of the world. When we look back at life over the millennia of which we have a history, we do not seem to have done so badly. Reasons and interpretations lie in a Darwinian world, in which we might hope that not only the big beasts, but also the *dulce et utile* – the agreeable and the useful – out-compete the others. We should toast our ancestors for getting us where we are, and since reason, the protectorate that philosophers police, is our concern, we must continually monitor the forces that lead us uphill or downhill, and have faith that the best will overcome the worst.

# NOTES

## 1. CORRESPONDENCE

1   Jeremy Bentham, *Deontology, Or The Science of Morality*, vol. 2, §52.
2   *Collected Papers of Charles Sanders Peirce*, vol. 8, Arthur W. Burks, ed., Cambridge: Harvard University Press, 1958, §112, p. 83.
3   Donald Davidson, 'Truth Rehabilitated', in Brandom, ed., *Rorty and his Critics*, Oxford: Blackwell, 2000, p. 66.
4   Richard Rorty, 'Texts and Lumps', in his *Philosophical Papers*, vol. 1, Cambridge: Cambridge University Press, p. 79; Peter Strawson, 'Truth', in *Proceedings of the Aristotelian Society* 1950, p. 129.
5   Brand Blanshard, *The Nature of Thought*, London: Allen & Unwin, 1939, vol. 2, p. 268.
6   Gottlob Frege, 'The Thought: A Logical Inquiry', *Mind*, vol. 65, 1956, p. 292.
7   William James, *Pragmatism*, New York: Longmans, Green & Co, 1907, p. 246.
8   William James, *Pragmatism*, p. 62.
9   James Leuba, 'Professor William James's Interpretation of Religious Experience', *International Journal of Ethics*, vol. 14, 1903, p. 331.

## 2. COHERENCE

10   John McDowell, *Mind and World*, Cambridge: Harvard University Press, 1996, p. 11.
11   Donald Davidson, 'A Coherence Theory of Truth and Knowledge', in Lepore, ed., *Truth and Interpretation: Perspectives on the Philosophy of Donald Davidson*, Oxford: Blackwell, 1986, p. 310.

## 3. PRAGMATISM

12  William James, *The Meaning of Truth*, New York: Longmans, Green & Co. 1927, p. 76.

13  C. S. Peirce, 'How to Make Our Ideas Clear', in *Chance, Love, and Logic*, Lincoln, Nebraska: Bison Books, 1998. Essay originally published in 1878.

14  William James, *The Meaning of Truth*, p. 189.

15  Sir Hugh Trevor-Roper, 'The Invention of Tradition: The Highland Tradition of Scotland', in *The Invention of Tradition*, Eric Hobsbawm & Terence Ranger, eds, Cambridge: Cambridge University Press, 1983. Of course the Scots are not alone. Myths of national glory are virtually inescapable.

16  William James, *Pragmatism*, p. 233.

17  *The Collected Papers of Charles Sanders Peirce*, vol. 5, Charles Harshorne & Paul Weiss, eds, Cambridge: Harvard University Press, 1934, §589, p. 412.

## 4. DEFLATIONISM

18  Harry Frankfurt, *On Bullshit*, Princeton: Princeton University Press, 2005.

## SUMMARY OF PART I

19  William James, *Pragmatism*, p. 197.

## 7. TRUTHS OF TASTE; TRUTH IN ART

20  Henry James, *Portraits of Places*, London: Macmillan, 1883. Unless otherwise signalled, the quotations from Henry James are from this essay.

21  T. S. Eliot, 'The Function of Criticism', in *The Complete Prose of T. S. Eliot, The Perfect Critic 1919–1926*, A. Cuda & R. Schuchard, eds, Baltimore: Johns Hopkins University Press, 2014, p. 459.

22  Hume, 'Of The Standard of Taste', in *Essays, Moral, Political and Literary*, vol. 1, Eugene F. Miller, ed., Indianapolis: Liberty Fund, p. 244.

23  R. G. Collingwood, *The Principles of Art*, Oxford: Oxford University Press, 1938, pp. 110f.
24  Ibid., pp. 125–53.

## 8. TRUTH IN ETHICS

25  David Hume, *Enquiry Concerning the Principles of Morals*, L. A. Selby-Bigge, ed., Oxford: Oxford University Press, 1975, §9, pp. 272–3.
26  David Hume, *Enquiry Concerning the Principles of Morals*, appendix 3, p. 306.

## 10. RELIGION AND TRUTH

27  The paragraphs that follow are owed to the scholarship and interpretation of Thomas Holden, 'Hobbes's First Cause', *Journal of the History of Philosophy*, vol. 53, no. 4, 2015, pp. 647–68.
28  Hobbes, *Leviathan*, London 1651, Rod Hay, ed., for the McMaster University Archive of the History of Economic Thought, xxxi, p. 223.
29  Hobbes, *Leviathan*, xlvi, p. 423.
30  Hobbes, *Critique du* De Mundo *de Thomas White*, J. Jacquot and H. W. Jones, eds, Paris: J. Vrin 1973, xxxv §16, p. 32.
31  Hume, *Enquiry Concerning Human Nature*, L. A. Selby-Bigge, ed., Oxford: Oxford University Press, 1975, §11, p. 142.

## 11. INTERPRETATIONS

32  Hobbes, *Leviathan*, xlvi, p. 427.

# FURTHER INVESTIGATIONS

Useful collections of classical readings and articles on truth include:

Blackburn, Simon, & Simmons, Keith (eds), *Truth*. Oxford: Oxford University Press (1999)

Horwich, Paul (ed.), *Theories of Truth*. New York: Dartmouth (1994)

Lynch, Michael P. (ed.), *The Nature of Truth: Classic and Contemporary Perspectives*. Boston: The MIT Press (2001)

Schmitt, Frederick F. (ed.), *Theories of Truth*. Oxford: Blackwell (2003)

A valuable account of some of the ways in which truth and falsity appeared problematic in classical philosophy is given in:

Denyer, Nicholas, *Language, Thought, and Falsehood in Ancient Greek Philosophy*. London: Routledge (1991)

It was only at the end of the nineteenth century that articles and books with truth itself as a topic began to proliferate. Although the British Idealists, particularly F. H. Bradley in his essay 'On Truth and Copying' (*Mind*, 1907) and H. H. Joachim in *The Nature of Truth* (Oxford: Oxford University Press, 1906), had powerfully attacked any correspondence theory, attempts to make it work included:

Russell, Bertrand, 'The Philosophy of Logical Atomism', in R. C. Marsh (ed.), *Logic and Knowledge*. London: Allen & Unwin (1956)

Wittgenstein, Ludwig, *Tractatus Logico-Philosophicus*. London: Routledge (1922)

In their hands, however, the correspondence theory required an involved and now discredited metaphysics. The idea of correspondence itself lives on, however, and later contributions include:

Armstrong, D. M., *A World of States of Affairs*. Cambridge: Cambridge University Press (1997)

Armstrong, D. M., *Truth and Truthmakers*. Cambridge: Cambridge University Press (2004)

The relation between correspondence and deflationary accounts of truth is explored in:

David, Marian, *Correspondence and Disquotation: An Essay on the Nature of Truth*. New York: Oxford University Press (1996)

Merricks, Trenton, *Truth and Ontology*. Oxford: Oxford University Press (2007)

In the philosophy of mathematics it is natural to suspect that there is no more to mathematical truth than provability, although technical results such as the famous incompleteness theorems of Kurt Gödel make this difficult to explain and defend. The essays collected in Michael Dummett's *Truth and Other Enigmas* (Oxford: Clarendon Press, 1978) revolve around applying a similar approach to the relation between truth in other areas and assertibility. There is a parallel between this approach, which is similar to Peirce's prioritisation of method over truth, and the ethical theory in which virtue is a more fundamental concept than any good that is achieved by its exercise. Each approach privileges process over product. A collection on this parallel is:

Battaly, Heather D. (ed.), *Virtue and Vice, Moral and Epistemic*. Oxford: Blackwell (2010)

Further work in Dummett's direction is found in Crispin Wright's *Truth and Objectivity* (Cambridge, MA: Harvard University Press, 1992). Wright's book also stimulated the view that different conceptions of truth could apply in different areas. A useful collection on this theme is:

Pedersen, Nikolai, & Wright, Cory (eds), *Truth and Pluralism: Current Debates*. Oxford: Oxford University Press (2013)

The earliest stirrings of a deflationary approach to truth can be found in Gottlob Frege's 'Thoughts', in his *Logical Investigations* (Oxford: Blackwell, 1977), and 'The thought: A Logical Inquiry' (*Mind* 65, 1956). F. P. Ramsey's paper 'Facts and Propositions' (*Aristotelian Society Supplementary Volume* 7, 1927) was another pioneering instance of the idea. Important later contributions include:

Horwich, Paul, *Truth*. Oxford: Blackwell (1990)
Quine, W. V. O., *Pursuit of Truth*. Harvard University Press (1992)

The idea of truth being indefinable was boosted by papers collected in:

Davidson, Donald, *Inquiries Into Truth and Interpretation*: *Philosophical Essays* vol. 2. Oxford: Oxford University Press (2001)

The Paradox of the Liar and its many offspring have generated a huge and generally technical literature. An accessible and interesting account can be found in:

Simmons, Keith, *Universality and the Liar: An Essay on Truth and the Diagonal Argument*. Cambridge: Cambridge University Press (1993)

The relevance of the theory of truth to modern or postmodern scepticism about the notion is explored in:

Blackburn, Simon, *Truth: A Guide for the Perplexed*. London: Allen Lane & Penguin (2005)
Nagel, Ernest, *The Last Word*. New York: Oxford University Press (1997)
Williams, Bernard, *Truth and Truthfulness*. Princeton: Princeton University Press (2002)

Truth is, inevitably, connected to issues in metaphysics and ontology. A useful wide-ranging collection is:

Chalmers, David, Manley, David, & Wasserman, Ryan (eds), *Metametaphysics: New Essays on the Foundations of Ontology*. New York: Oxford University Press (2009)

Internet resources on the topic of truth include the Stanford Encyclopedia of Philosophy at http://plato.stanford.edu/, and the Philosophical Papers site at http://philpapers.org/. A video classic is the conversation between Sir Peter Strawson and Gareth Evans from 1973: Part 1 is at https://www.youtube.com/watch?v=BLV-eYacfbE and Part 2 at https://www.youtube.com/watch?v=w__pIcl_1rs. The interviews recorded at http://www.philosophybites.com/ make another excellent resource for people finding their way into philosophy.

# INDEX

# *IDEAS* IN PROFILE
## SMALL INTRODUCTIONS TO BIG TOPICS

*Ideas in Profile* is a landmark series that offers concise and entertaining introductions to topics that matter.

### ALREADY PUBLISHED

*The Ancient World* Jerry Toner
*Art in History* Martin Kemp
*Criticism* Catherine Belsey
*Geography* Carl Lee and Danny Dorling
*Music* Andrew Gant
*Politics* David Runciman
*Shakespeare* Paul Edmondson
*Social Theory* William Outhwaite
*Theories of Everything* Frank Close

### FORTHCOMING

*Conservatism* Roger Scruton
*Feminism* Deborah Cameron
*Language* Alexandra Aikhenvald
*Socialism* Mark Stears